Great Aunt Alice
and the Black Camel
Diana Fletcher

ISBN: 978-1-8383998-0-1

eBook: 978-1-8383998-1-8

Cover and text design: Konstantinos Vasdekis

Back cover and text illustrations: Mia Buckton

Printed and bound in Great Britain

10 9 8 7 6 5 4 3 2 1

For the Bedouin and their Camels

— Contents —

— Chapter 1 —

Great
Aunt Alice

Early each morning, Great Aunt Alice woke to the sound of cockerels crowing in her village, reminding her that another day had dawned on the magical island of Djerba. She was especially happy today, as her Great Niece Georgina, known as George, and her Great Nephew Freddie, known as Fred, were coming to stay with her for their Easter holidays. They would be the first members of the family she had left behind in England, to see the new home she had chosen in the North African country of Tunisia.

Her rambling old house was built around a courtyard and the rooms were all on the same level, which meant she did not have to climb any stairs. She was now seventy years old and suffered from a wonky ankle which had never fully recovered after breaking it in a horse-riding accident in London's Hyde Park. She had now retired from working in the busy city, where her tiny flat was not much bigger than a giant rabbit hutch. But because it was in the centre of town and next to Pimlico tube station she had been able to sell it for enough money (with some left over) to begin a new adventure living on her most favourite continent: Africa. Her garden was full of tortoises, seven to be precise, which she had named after the colours of the rainbow: Red, Orange, Yellow, Green, Blue, Indigo and Violet. The only way she could tell one from the other was by dobbing the appropriate blob of coloured paint onto their shells. She had rescued these sweet creatures from a market stall in Houmt Souk, where she did her shopping once a week. She saw them clambering helplessly over each other, imprisoned in a plastic crate with only rotten lettuce leaves to eat. She had wanted to give them the chance to escape to a new life, just has she had done.

Her house and garden quickly became a haven to all sorts of other animals and birds – Kitton, a black and white stray cat whom she found roaming the dusty streets of her village; Merlin the Macaw who flew in from nowhere, landing on a bowl of oranges in the centre of her wooden kitchen table where he decided to take up semi-permanent residence; alternatively perching high up on a palm tree in the garden keeping a beady eye on what went on outside. Large golden fish swam in the courtyard fountain – thankfully too big for Kitton to eat – and an ornate birdcage hanging from the fig tree protected the two budgerigars Bertie and Beatrice from Kitton's grasping claws.

Great Aunt Alice had decided to grow old gracefully. She had once been told by a Touareg Chieftain whom she had met in Timbuktu, that every age has its beauty. She had not been sad to part with her smart London outfits and shoes, and now enjoyed the freedom of wearing clothes to suit her very own new age of bohemian beauty. She kept her wardrobe simple: long tunics worn over narrow trousers in the day; colourful kaftans worn over leggings in the evening. A dab of lipstick and a generous sweep of blusher powder for her cheeks was all she needed in the way of make-up, and she loved her colourful collection of chunky ethnic jewellery. Her only indulgence was scarves – she was never seen without one, whether draped around her shoulders, wrapped around her head, or simply tied at the neck. There were mohair wool ones to keep her warm in winter, and cotton ones to protect her from the sun in summer, when she often plonked a traditional Djerbian woven straw hat on top. And she always wore spectacles. She owned two pairs, one with thick purple frames, the other with thick sky-blue frames; these could not be left behind in London. She was as blind as a bat without them, and her trendy opticians, Opera Opera in Covent Garden wanted to prove to her that poor eyesight need not be boring – treat yourself to some whacky eyewear and have fun they said. The lenses were so clever that they went dark in the sun, so one way and another, her glasses were an essential item.

Great Aunt Alice was a keen photographer. She had shipped over her cameras and photograph albums, as well as heaps of loose photographs from her travels which she intended to turn into a very special photographic library. The oil paintings and watercolours that had hung on the walls of her London flat were the only other things to have been shipped over – everything else in her Tunisian house had been bought locally.

— Chapter 2 —

George
and Fred

George (aged twelve) and Fred (nine) felt like grown-ups. It was the first time they had ever flown in an aeroplane. Their Mum and Dad had waved goodbye to them at Exeter airport, where they had been introduced to a kind and gentle air hostess called Caroline who would look after them right up to the moment she handed the children over to Great Aunt Alice at Djerba airport. Soon after take-off, Fred felt sick, but quickly recovered when the in-flight movie began and the lunchtime sandwiches arrived on the folding table in front of him. Sensible sister George instructed him to keep his seatbelt fastened throughout the four-hour journey, and to set a good example she did the same. Most importantly, she did not want to let on to Fred that she was feeling a little bit frightened of being so high up in the air with nothing but cotton wool clouds below and a brilliant blue sky above. To calm her nerves she drank Coca Cola through a straw, and concentrated on the film *ET* all about an extra-terrestrial being coming down to planet earth where a little boy befriended him, and after a string of exciting adventures together, helped him to return to his home planet.

When the film ended, a stewardess came round to make sure their seat belts were firmly secured, as the plane had begun its descent through a mass of dense cloud which caused it to rock from side to side. The pilot warned the passengers through his public address system to prepare for a bumpy landing due to turbulent conditions. George and Fred held hands and shut their eyes. The next thing they knew was that everyone was clapping and cheering, the traditional way of saying thank you to the captain and his crew for a safe landing. Because the two children were under the special care of Caroline the air hostess, they were the very first to make their way down the steep rickety steps that had been wheeled up to the front entrance of the plane. They made sure they had all their hand luggage with them. George felt responsible for Fred. Being the elder of the two made her feel important. She had to make sure they carried their passports with them wherever they went and kept these in a zipped compartment of her rucksack alongside the mobile phone she had been given for her twelfth birthday.

A warm wind blew across the tarmac as they stepped onto the airport bus which ferried them to the Arrivals terminal. Caroline ushered them through passport control where they handed over the forms they had filled in, showing the man at the desk their passports. The next thing was to collect their baggage off the carousel. Caroline found a trolley and helped load their two brightly labelled suitcases which happily appeared into view almost immediately. George and Fred were beside themselves with excitement, but a little bit nervous too. The last time they had seen Great Aunt Alice was three years ago when she was still living in London. Would they recognise her?

A jostling crowd of men, women and children were waiting impatiently on the other side of the barrier in the vast marbled Arrivals hall to be reunited with their loved ones. Standing well back from the noisy confusion of people trying to find each other, Fred spotted a solitary figure standing underneath the Exit sign – he nudged George – 'Do you think that could be her?' 'It can't be,' replied George, 'I can't ever remember Great Aunt Alice looking like that.' With Caroline's help they pushed the trolley towards the far side of the hall. As they got closer to this extraordinary looking person, wearing what looked like a long evening dress in tangerine silk, and a gold scarf wound around her head and shoulders, to their astonishment they saw she was holding up a miniature blackboard with 'George and Fred' chalked across it in spidery writing.

'Hello darlings,' she cried in an embarrassingly loud voice as she swept towards them, arms outstretched. Fred was not good at receiving or giving hugs, but George made up for his shyness by planting two affectionate kisses on Great Aunt Alice's cheeks, taking great care not to knock off her large blue framed spectacles or become entangled in the rows of multi-coloured beads that hung almost down to her waist. She smelt delicious, of orange blossom and roses, and reminded George of the nursery rhyme Ride a Cock Horse to Banbury Cross:

'With rings on her fingers and bells on her toes, she shall have music wherever she goes'. Great Aunt Alice's elegant fingers were adorned with silver rings on one hand, and gold on the other, with an assortment of bangles to match. As George would later discover, and much to her delight, every evening Great Aunt Alice changed out of her boring trainers, and into soft leather sandals, with tinkling bells stitched into their curling toes!

Great Aunt Alice thanked Caroline for being so kind to George and Fred, and beckoned to her taxi driver, Kador. All the taxis were bright yellow, and each one had its own number on the front of the roof – Kador's was 431. Great Aunt Alice did not have her own car, and there was usually a task or two for him to do on most days of the week. Today's was to drive to the airport, collect the children, help with their luggage, and take them all back to her house in Erriadh. She had named her beloved new home Dar Karmous, which translated from Arabic into English means 'House of the Fig'. Finding the right house to buy had taken her months, but the moment she had stepped from the hot dusty street and into the welcomingly cool courtyard, with its dominant fig tree and cascading fountain, she knew she had finally found the place of her dreams.

George and Fred climbed out of the taxi and found themselves in another world. They were at once introduced to the gardener and housekeeper, Mustapha, who wore a long grey overall, and on his head, not one hat, but two: a round red felt fez to keep him warm, and a traditional Djerbian straw wide brimmed hat to keep him cool. He began his working day wearing both, and depending on how hot or cold it was, ended up wearing one or the other. He was about eighty, bent like an ancient gnarled olive tree that had weathered strong salty winds blown inland from the sea. His handsome old face, deeply wrinkled, featured a large beak-like nose, a toothless smile, and knowing twinkling eyes. He showed George and Fred to their room, Kador following with the luggage. The children were gobsmacked! Their beds were set back in arched alcoves at opposite ends of the room – it was as if they each had their own private lantern-lit cave. The mattresses they would sleep on rested on raised stone plinths, with pillows and cushions neatly arranged on top of the cream bed linen. Colourful Berber rugs woven from camel, sheep and goat hair adorned the terracotta tiled floor, big painted wooden chests would provide storage for their clothes, and a round marble topped table on slender curvaceous metal legs with chairs to match – the perfect place for them to attempt to write their journals.

— Chapter 3 —

Dar Karmous
and Hotel Marhaba

George and Fred barely slept at all on their first night at Dar Karmous. There were far too many exciting things to talk about. They adored the rambling old house. Fred lost no time in working out his own special name for it, Dark Mouse, which made him giggle. George thought it would be a great idea to turn Fred's funny joke into their very own secret password. Little did they know what a wise decision this would be...

They had unpacked soon after their arrival, and Mustapha was anxious for them to meet the animals and birds before it got too dark. They had already met Merlin the Macaw, perched on the bowl of oranges at the centre of the kitchen table, but there was just enough time for a tortoise hunt in the garden, and to work out the names of each one from the blobs of different coloured paint on their shells. They then counted the plump fish swimming in the fountain, before stroking Kitton, who was sitting under the birdcage where Bertie and Beatrice the budgies were roosting. They were easy to tell apart – Bertie had violet feathers, and Beatrice emerald green ones. There was something mysterious about the black and white Kitton – his ears were bent and battered from fights with other cats, and judging by his wise old scarred face, George and Fred were convinced he had a great many stories to tell, if only he could speak.... Fred was certain that Kitton would approve of his Dark Mouse joke.

After their almost sleepless night, George and Fred enjoyed a scrumptious breakfast of scrambled eggs, croissants, fig jam and freshly squeezed orange juice. Although Great Aunt Alice found cooking an effort, she was clever at choosing the very best ingredients, and had the knack of making everything look attractive. Dark blue pottery jugs of yellow roses decorated the long kitchen table, of which Merlin was the colourful squawking centrepiece. George and Fred did not let on that they had been talking all night. When Great Aunt Alice asked them what sort of things they would like to do during their holidays, they were able to answer straight away that what they wanted most of all was to spend as much time as possible on the beach. Their suggestion was met with open arms – George and Fred had always been water babies and had grown into strong confident swimmers. They had brought their flippers and snorkels with them, plus floppy sunhats and oceans of sun lotion. Everything they needed for their first day by the sea was crammed into a large basket made out of woven palm tree leaves. Great Aunt Alice rang straight away for Kador in his yellow taxi and asked him to take them all to the Hotel Marhaba, a fifteen-minute drive from Erriadh. She loved this charming little hotel by the seashore and knew all the people who worked there. It had become her home from home, as whenever she did not have enough space in her own house for friends to stay, or they wanted to be by the sea, this was where she sent them, knowing that they would be beautifully looked after.

When they got to the hotel, Great Aunt Alice was warmly welcomed by Amal the manageress, and arrangements were made for the children to have lunch every day by the garden swimming pool, under the shade of the straw umbrellas. Amal also arranged for them to have their own locker in the staff room where they could safely leave their belongings whilst they were out and about. A narrow sandy path zig zagged its way from the garden down to the beach – George and Fred couldn't wait to start exploring on their own! They would return to Dar Karmous at the end of each day, Kador collecting them in Taxi 431. George had already tapped his mobile number into her own phone, plus the number for Great Aunt Alice who was now on her way back home with Kador.

George and Fred wasted no time in changing into their bathing costumes, George carefully fastening the locker key to hers with a safety pin. They would read their books and take photographs after lunch when it would be far too hot to do much else. But right now they wanted to make the most of the cooler part of the day. They hurried single file down the sandy path, and raced each other into the sea, squealing with delight. The flippers and snorkels could wait until tomorrow when they would have a much better idea of the safest places to swim, and where the beefy lifeguards were based.

After much splashing in the salty water, their attention was drawn to a camel train padding (not paddling!) along the beach. There were three large caramel coloured camels, and a fluffy white baby one trailing behind, desperately trying to keep up with the long, loping strides of his elders, who were roped together in a long line. The camel at the front was being led by a man dressed in a dark blue, gold embroidered long sleeved tunic over dark blue baggy trousers, embroidered at the ankle; an exotic black turban was wound around his head. 'Come on Fred, let's go and say hello, and maybe their owner will let us ride them.' 'Great idea,' said Fred, 'especially as we have never ridden one before.' And off they went to speak to the owner. His name was Monir. He had a lean handsome face, a sparkling smile and friendly brown eyes. The camels too looked friendly, and were in good condition, well fed, with soft furry coats. 'Would it be possible for us to have a ride?' enquired George. 'But of course,' replied Monir, 'but there will be a charge of fifteen dinars each for half an hour.' 'Oh crikey,' said George 'I've left the money Great Aunt Alice gave us in the locker at the hotel, I will run and get it.'

She sped back to the hotel, collected thirty dinars from her purse, and when she returned, found the camels couched down, their long legs folded underneath their tummies. Apart from the baby camel, they all had saddles on their backs, with a metal bar at the front to hold on to. Fred was the first one to climb aboard. He'd chosen the leading camel, called Ali Baba, and George watched anxiously as his mount lurched to its feet, Fred holding on to the front of the saddle for dear life. It was a long way up! Then it was George's turn to get onto her camel, Lazarak, who rested patiently on the sand until she was confident enough for him to rise steadily to his feet. Monir treated his camels gently, whispering to them as they strode along, at the same time constantly checking that the children were happy and not afraid. He need not have worried – they were enjoying every single second of their new experience. The fact that they were used to riding ponies in England was an advantage. The biggest difference though was the height of these magnificent beasts – if for any reason the worst should happen, it was an awful long way down to fall! But the children did have a natural sense of balance, which would serve them well if the camels got into any kind of trouble.

All too soon their ride came to an end, but getting off the camels was scary. Monir told them to hold on very tightly to the front of their saddles. He carefully explained that the camels go down part of the way on their front legs, and then all the way on their back legs, before going down the rest of the way on their front legs! 'This is much more difficult than getting off a pony,' mumbled Fred who had turned rather pale. 'It will be fine,' said George. 'Just do what

Monir tells you – in a way it's much easier than getting on and off ponies, because at least the camels kneel all the way down to the ground for us – you won't get ponies to do that!' Fred closed his eyes and hoped for the best. He need not have worried – Monir had one firm hand on the camel's head collar rope, and the other on Fred's knee. He did the same when it came to George's turn. They both landed safely, pleased with themselves. 'Let's do this again tomorrow, and the next day, and then the one after that!' said Fred confidently. 'I agree,' replied George. 'I think a ride most days would be terrific and we can try to improve our getting on and off skills. But now it's time for something to eat, I'm starving.' They said goodbye to Monir, and walked slowly back to the hotel, searching for pretty shells as they went – these would make a nice present for Great Aunt Alice who loved to collect things.

Sitting in the garden under a giant straw umbrella, drinking Coca Cola through a straw and dipping chunky chips into a bowl of tomato sauce was George and Fred's idea of bliss. It was now very hot, and the lovely thoughtful Amal suggested that an ice cream to finish would cool them down. George and Fred abandoned the idea of spending the rest of the afternoon at the beach, instead collecting the basket from their locker. They decided to leave the bulky goggles and flippers behind at the hotel throughout their Easter holidays. They climbed into their shorts, shirts and sandals, put a comb through their hair, and called Kador. The thought of reading their books in the comfort of their cave-like bedroom at Dar Karmous was irresistible, and it would be nice to be back in good time, so they could chat to Great Aunt Alice and get to know the animals better.

— Chapter 4 —

Talking
to the Animals

Mustapha, wearing his Djerbian sun hat, was at the courtyard door to greet them. He unloaded the children's basket from the boot of the taxi, and thanked Kador for getting them home. Great Aunt Alice was having her afternoon nap. The children followed Mustapha to their room on tip toes so as not to wake her up. 'I think I feel like a bit of a nap too,' said Fred. 'Well I think you should have a shower first and put on your towelling dressing gown before burrowing into your private cave. I will do the same once you've finished, but now I'm going to read my book,' replied George. The bathrooms here were known as wet rooms. The floors were tiled, the walls marbled, and although of course there were loos and basins, there were no bathtubs in the guest rooms. The water cascaded down like a torrential rainstorm from huge fixed showerheads. The one and only bathtub to be found at Dar Karmous was in Great Aunt Alice's wet room. She adored relaxing in a foaming froth of gorgeous smelling bubbles, listening to the radio, with a glass of wine at her fingertips, a luxury she treated herself to each evening before changing for dinner. George and Fred thought their shower was the best thing ever, the quickest way of getting clean. Lolling in a bath would be a complete waste of time for them – there were too many exciting things to do and talk about.

After an hour or so of peace and quiet, the children got properly dressed and went out into the garden. Kitton was sitting under the fig tree, and Merlin was perched way up high on his usual lookout place at the top of the swaying date palm. It was important for him to keep watch over what was going on outside, and every day before bedtime he and Kitton would get together to talk about what he had seen and heard. Merlin the bird was not afraid of Kitton the cat – I think it was more the other way round, since Merlin was very large with a sharp curving beak and wide spreading claws that would be capable of picking Kitton up in a flash were he to put a whisker out of place. They agreed a long while ago that they would be friends, and they made a good team. Kitton walked stealthily towards George and Fred, and to their astonishment began talking to them in a mixture of miaows and words.

'Did you hear that George? He asked how we were, and did we like Tunisia?'

'Yes, I did,' replied George. 'I can hardly believe my ears! We must tell him at once that we do love Tunisia, and that we want to learn as much as we can about it. Do you realise that now we have discovered we can more or less speak the same language, a whole new world has opened up for us?' 'I sure do,' burbled Fred in a mild state of shock, 'and do you suppose he talks like this to Great Aunt Alice and Mustapha?' 'There's only one way to find out, Fred, we must ask him!'

Kitton explained that this secret language was known as Noah. It was taught to animals at The Ark evening classes in towns and villages all over Tunisia. It could only be understood by children. Quite a lot of animals had learnt how to speak it, but most had found the homework too hard, especially the donkeys and mules who were so tired at the end of the day after pulling carts and carrying heavy loads that the last thing they wanted to do was to trot off to these evening classes. They simply longed for three things: a thirst-quenching drink of water, a feed of corn, and a good night's sleep. Anything else was too much for them. It was much easier for birds and cats to attend lessons, because they were pets rather than workers and were free to fly and roam.

George and Fred decided to keep this extraordinary information to themselves – besides, Great Aunt Alice would never believe such a tale, and would put it down to sunstroke which often made people feel rather peculiar. It was nearly time for supper, and they asked Kitton and Merlin if they could come and talk to them tomorrow evening, same time, same place.

Great Aunt Alice's homely kitchen is where all the important things happened: cooking, eating, chatting, making plans and telling stories. This evening they all sat down to a huge dish of steamed couscous, a North African dish of coarsely ground pasta made from semolina, covered in a scrumptious sauce of vegetables, chicken, herbs and spices. Great Aunt Alice had taken great care not to overdo the spices for the children. Besides, she always kept a jar of Harissa – a fiery hot red sauce made from chillis – next to the salt and pepper pots, so that she could spoon this onto her plate to her own taste.

The kitchen was in the west wing of the house, and George and Fred's bedroom in the east wing. Great Aunt Alice's rooms were in the longest part of the old rambling building that joined these two wings together. When it was time to go to bed, George and Fred walked across the courtyard, past the tinkling fountain, and unlocked the heavy wooden door into their place, which they had grandly nicknamed The Haven Apartment. Great Aunt Alice had given them a key of their own, so that they were free to come and go as they pleased without having to bother anyone. Their bedroom window looked out onto Kitton's fig tree and Merlin's date palm which meant the children could whisper goodnight to their furry and feathered friends without disturbing their Great Aunt. At supper, they had told her about their camel riding on the beach and asked if they could please do the same again tomorrow. They explained they would be perfectly happy to go there and back in Kador's yellow taxi on their own, there was no need for anyone to accompany them, and in any case there was always dear kind Amal to help them if they got into any difficulties, as they would of course be having lunch in the Hotel Marhaba garden under her watchful eye.

— Chapter 5 —

Zeydoun
and Lashkar

The children slept well. There was no need for an alarm clock to wake them, because if the early morning chorus of crowing cockerels failed to do so, then the sound of Mustapha sweeping the courtyard certainly would. It was a task that he began soon after sunrise, before going down to the village to buy fresh bread (known out here as baguettes) for breakfast. He lived in a tiny house tucked away in the corner of the vegetable garden. This gentle, sweet man was proud of his daily routine of sweeping, shopping, gardening, and caring for Great Aunt Alice who was a real treasure, never, ever taking him for granted. They shared lots of the daily chores as well as the village gossip!

When George and Fred returned to their Haven Apartment after breakfast, they were amazed to find the beds made, the wet room sparkling, the towels neatly folded, the tiled floors mopped, and the furniture dusted. To complete the scene, an earthenware bowl of pink scented roses had been placed on the bench under the mirror in the little entrance hall. They felt terribly guilty that this dear old man had gone to so much trouble, because at home they were expected to help with all the housework, and they told Mustapha that they would like to do exactly the same for him out here. But he would not hear of it – he just wanted them to enjoy themselves and to have a lovely time.

George and Fred wound down the window of Taxi 431 to wave goodbye to Great Aunt Alice as she saw them on their way. She blew them kisses in return, her silver and gold rings catching the morning sunlight. Although she did not believe in making endless boring rules that started off with 'don't do this' and 'you must not do that', there were certain things she was extremely strict about, particularly that George did not leave the house without her fully charged mobile phone. If it needed topping up during the day, she explained, then Amal would see to it. George took this responsibility very seriously.

The children quickly discovered that as well as speaking Arabic (a load of gobbledygook to them) Kador also spoke French, which meant they could practise what they had learnt at school from Madame Felice, their French teacher. Although they spoke slowly, and with an English accent, he had no difficulty understanding them. They found the same thing with the Hotel Marhaba staff, as well as the camel men on the beach, which was really useful.

'Good morning children,' said Amal 'Did you sleep well?'

'Goodness me yes,' replied George, 'like logs, and now we're longing to go down to the beach and ride the camels.'

'That's a great plan for the morning,' said Amal. 'Here is your locker key – leave anything you don't want to take with you behind, and I will keep a table for you at lunchtime, just like yesterday.' 'Thank you, Amal, you are so kind to us,' said George, before marching off to the staff room with Fred to sort out their stuff.

They felt as free as air, running barefoot in the sand, the cool sea breeze blowing through their hair, their faces turned towards the sun, a golden orb of energy! This was the life - no school, no nagging parents, no homework, and no chilly rain-soaked holidays or mackintoshes! Just when they thought things couldn't get any better, they saw smiling Monir walking towards them, his train of happy, contented camels strung out behind him.

'Hurrah,' yelled Fred, 'George, did you remember to bring the dinars with you to pay for our ride?'

'Yes, I've got them with me, and you never know, if we offer to help Monir groom his camels, he may even give us a slightly reduced price, but we can talk that over with him later on – after all, we're here for several weeks.' 'Good idea,' said Fred.

Monir was as pleased to see the children as they were to see him. He commanded his camels to kneel, and after a little encouragement, they slowly folded up their long legs and down they went onto the sandy floor below. He helped Fred get on Ali Baba, and afterwards it was George's turn to be helped on to Lazarak. Getting on the second time round was much easier than the first, provided you remembered not to let go of the iron bar in front of the saddle. Monir made sure that the children were sitting firmly in their saddles before setting off. They still hadn't got used to being so far from the ground, but were much less scared than yesterday, feeling confident enough to ask Monir if he could please take them for a much longer ride this morning. He agreed. Today they would go on a proper trek, the full length of the curving seashore.

Riding camels reminded George and Fred of sitting on the top deck of a double decker bus. They could see for miles ahead and invented a competition as to which seaside hotel had the prettiest garden. They had the most brilliant view of everything and everyone, noticing things they would never have seen had they been walking along on their own feet. Even if they had chosen to ride the glossy coated Arab ponies that were popular with lots of beach goers, the view would not have been half as good.

Fred seemed to be concentrating hard on something or other in the distance. This was unusual for him, as more often than not, he preferred to drift in and out of his own dream world. He had already decided he wanted to be an actor when he grew up, whilst his sister had set her heart on becoming a musician.

George did not like missing out on anything. 'What's up?' she asked her brother.

'See those jagged rocks over there,' replied Fred, 'the ones jutting out into the sea, I thought I saw what looked like a camel's face peeping over the top of them, looking in our direction, but whatever it was has disappeared.'

'All I can see are a few seagulls strutting about,' said George, 'but wait, I think I can hear someone shouting.' At that very moment, the air was filled with the sound of flapping wings and screeches as the birds took flight – or was it fright?

As they got closer to the rocks, Ali Baba and Lazarak began twitching their ears backwards and forwards and making peculiar gurgling noises. Camels are every bit as clever as guard dogs, being able to see, hear and smell things long before their owners and riders can. Monir's gentle dromedaries had sensed danger.

The tide was in, and to get to the beach on the other side of the rocks meant wading out to sea. Monir rolled up his trousers, and checked that his four camels were securely roped to each other before warning the children to sit tight. Fred was at the front of the train, then George, with the two other riderless camels, Llama and Lahajah, following on behind.

The ships of the desert were briefly about to become ships of the sea as they ventured into the water, treading carefully as they went. They were not afraid, trusting their master. Besides, the occasional wash in salty water was good for their padded feet and furry legs, getting rid of any nasty insects that might have set up home there!

As the camels sploshed their way through the waves, the shouts grew louder. When they finally clambered on to the beach at the far side of the rocks, Ali Baba and Lazarak swished their tails violently – a sure sign that all was not well. It was then that the children saw for themselves the reason.

Huddled together were two terrified camels trying desperately to shield each other from the sharp blows they were receiving from their owner, who thought that beating them with a stick would make them do exactly what he wanted. George and Fred were horrified. They asked Monir if they could dismount, and would he please go and tell this horrible man to put down his stick, whilst they went over to comfort the camels.

Monir too was shocked. He had never seen the man before. He decided the safest way of approaching such a nasty looking stranger was to offer him a cigarette. This turned out to be a clever move, since it did not take him long to find out that the man's name was Mokhtar. His tobacco stained lips, teeth and fingers left no doubt that smoking was the man's favourite pastime, and a good way of distracting him from beating the camels.

The pungent smell of tobacco smoke wafted across to the spot where Mokhtar's camels cowered. But it was not the smoke that caused the tears to flow from the camels' sad brown eyes. George and Fred would soon discover that these were two desperately unhappy creatures. The larger one was black, and the smaller one white. They were both pitifully thin.

'What on earth can we do to help them?' cried George to Fred. Her question was answered, but to her astonishment, not by Fred.

The black camel slowly lowered his handsome head and whispered, 'I believe children can understand Noah, the language we learnt at evening classes in Sabria, our village in the Sahara Desert where we used to live so happily. My name is Zeydoun, and my friend is called Lashkar. I will do my best to explain how we got here.'

'Goodness me,' said Fred excitedly, trying very hard to keep his voice down, 'we are so glad we have found you, and yes, we do understand every word you are saying as we've heard Noah spoken by the animals who live at Great Aunt Alice's house in Erriadh, where we are spending our holidays.'

'This is the best news I have heard for weeks,' said Zeydoun. 'Let me tell you our story'. And with his long dark eyelashes, he blinked away the tears that were now falling uncontrollably down his cheeks. Luckily Mokhtar had lost interest in the attention the children were paying to Zeydoun and Lashkar, too busy greedily puffing away at Monir's cigarettes.

'Let me begin at the beginning,' said Zeydoun, lowering himself gently to the ground. Lashkar did the same, and the children sat down opposite them, pulling their floppy sunhats down over their heads. The camels were used to the sun but were constantly bothered by the hundreds of flies that clustered around the bleeding wounds where they had been beaten.

'All our lives, until just a few months ago, we belonged to a sweet, gentle young man called Khairi, who loved us and looked after us. His family kept chickens, rabbits, sheep, goats, horses, mules and camels. They were the people of the desert, known as the Bedouin. In return for their kindness and care, we were asked to carry tourists on our backs for trips into the Sahara. They came from England, Germany, Italy, Spain, France, Russia and sometimes from as far away as icy Finland. As I was the strongest camel, I had to carry the heaviest tourists, but I was never overloaded. Lashkar, who is smaller than me, was a great favourite with the children especially as he was white; he was also a racing camel, and every December, Khairi would ride him in the marathon at the Douz Festival where he nearly always came first. But when children rode him, he never went faster than a walk. The visitors paid Khairi to take them on these desert tours, which meant he had enough money to buy food, clothing, and to finish paying for the house he had built for his family.

Although it was too hot to work in the summer, we were always busy in the autumn, winter and spring months, often joining up with other desert guides and their camels, travelling for fifteen days at a time. Occasionally, a stalwart mule pulling a cart would come along too. He belonged to Cessia, Khairi's mother. We got on very well with the mule, especially as his cart carried most of the tourists' luggage, making our loads much lighter! Khairi did the cooking on these tours, and packed our huge saddle bags with all the food, bottled water, pots and pans he needed for the entire trip. He never forgot to include the sacks of corn for our evening feed, even though he made certain our overnight stops were at places where there were plenty of delicious herbs for us to eat. Our favourite herb was a tall grass known as Sabat.'

'So how did all this come to an end?' enquired George. 'I can't think of anything more thrilling than going on a desert adventure with you, Lashkar, Khairi and his mother's mule.'

'Fewer and fewer visitors came to the desert which meant less and less money for Khairi. He knew that sooner or later he would not have enough to buy our food which was getting more and more expensive. We would have to be sold. He could not afford to keep us any longer, and this made him very sad. A dealer in the village had offered him a good price, promising he would find a nice home for us. This turned out to be a lie. After a terrifying seven-hour journey crouched down in the back of a dirty old open truck, the dealer unloaded us onto the side of a stony road and made a call from his mobile. The next thing we knew was that we were being handed over to our new owner – Mokhtar!'

'No wonder you are feeling homesick,' said George.

'We are,' said Zeydoun. 'Unbearably so, and I am worried about poor Lashkar who is getting weaker each day. He is not as strong as me, and his back is covered in sores from a badly fitting saddle. We are both made to work from sunrise to sunset – there is no shortage of visitors on the island of Djerba. I have to carry the biggest ones, maybe three at a time, and Lashkar usually ends up carrying two or three squabbling children.'

George looked at Fred. 'There is only one thing for it – we must find a way of getting these camels back to where they belong – Sabria. This evening, we will talk to Kitton and Merlin, and see if between us, we can come up with some sort of plan.'

Monir waved to the children – he had managed to find out quite a lot about Mokhtar. Hanging around any longer would make the man suspicious. It was time to go.

— Chapter 6 —

Plans
Afoot

When George and Fred got back to Dar Karmous, Great Aunt Alice was waiting for them in the courtyard. 'I am so sorry my darlings, but I've got the most terrible toothache. I am in agony. Luckily my dentist in Tunis can see me the day after tomorrow, and I've asked my dear friend Belgacem to take me there and back in his comfortable Toyota truck. It is a seven-hour journey, and I shall spend two nights in Tunis which gives me the chance to do some shopping. I will stop off in Kairouan on the way home to buy some rugs and carpets for the house. Mustapha will look after you, and his daughter Nejwa will come and stay here with her little boy Hamdi until I get back. She will enjoy cooking in my kitchen, and Hamdi will love playing with the tortoises.'

'Oh you poor thing,' said George 'but please don't worry about us, we'll be fine. We've made great friends with Kador and Amal, and have got our days on the beach very well organised, especially as we've got to know Monir and his camels – we did a very long ride with him today, and we're getting much braver at the getting on and off bit.'

'That all sounds excellent,' said Great Aunt Alice. 'I am now going to have some painkillers and a rest on my bed before getting the supper together. Shall we meet in the kitchen at around 7pm?'

'Perfect,' said Fred. 'That will give us plenty of time to get ready and to catch up with writing our journals.'

The children desperately needed this time to themselves. They had not forgotten their early evening appointment with Kitton and Merlin – there was so much to tell them. They showered and dressed at great speed, picked up their journals, locked the door of their apartment behind them, and walked over to the fig tree, where they found Kitton stretched out under its leafy branches, and Merlin perched on the highest one. Merlin never liked being on the ground – the nearest he got to such a risky level was perching on the bowl of oranges in Great Aunt Alice's kitchen, which was a risk worth taking, as every day she gave him his very own dish of fruit, nuts and seeds.

Kitton was on tenterhooks to hear George and Fred's news – his feline instinct told him that something important had happened to them since their last meeting. He sat up, licked his front paws, and twisting his tail from side to side, waited for one of them to speak. He did not have long to wait...

'Kitton, Merlin, please, please, we need your help,' cried George. 'We've found two very homesick camels on the beach. Up until a few months ago, they had never, ever been parted from their gentle Bedouin owner Khairi, but he had to sell them because he no longer had enough money to buy food for them. It broke his heart, and his camels' hearts too. The dealer had promised that they would go to a good home – but that was a lie. They have been sold on to a cruel man called Mokhtar, and somehow we have to find a way of getting them back to where they have always belonged – Sabria.'

'How on earth did you find all this out?' growled Kitton. 'I'm sure it wasn't from Mokhtar.' 'No, no it wasn't,' replied George, 'it was from the camels themselves, Zeydoun and Lashkar, who both speak Noah. They were students at The Ark evening classes in Sabria.'

'Well that gives us a good start,' said Kitton. 'I will ask Merlin to fly down to the coast tonight, and he will speak to the Beachcomber Cats. These clever cats will be able to find out where Mokhtar keeps his camels at night. They know just about everything that goes on down there.'

Merlin, his head cocked to one side, took in every word that was being said; the moment he received final instructions from Kitton, he would be off. With a fair wind, he would get back before the children went to bed. In any case, their bedroom window looked out onto the fig tree, so it would be easy to wake them by tapping his beak against the window bars.

Kitton leapt onto the bottom branch of the fig tree. He was an agile climber, and in a matter of seconds had zig-zagged his way to the uppermost branch where Merlin was waiting for him.

'What an unhappy tale,' squawked Merlin, 'but your friends the Beachcomber Cats are intelligent spies, and I will ask them on your behalf to gather as much information as they can about the whereabouts of the horrible Mokhtar and where he tethers those poor camels. We can then all put our heads together and try to work out some sort of rescue plan.'

'Exactly,' muttered Kitton. 'None of this is going to be easy, but the children are determined, and we must do everything in our power to help them. I will see you later – good luck!'

Without making a sound, Merlin vanished into the evening sky, his blue and gold feathers every bit as colourful as the glorious violet sunset. Kitton climbed down to join the children under the tree.

'What is happening?' asked Fred.

'Merlin is on his way to the coast to meet the Beachcomber Cats. If all goes well, he should be back before you go to bed.'

'I'm so excited,' exclaimed George 'but at the same time, I'm scared.' Her tummy was turning somersaults. Fred had gone quiet.

Kitton decided to distract the children's attention with a loud miaow: 'Why don't you do a tortoise count – Great Aunt Alice makes a habit of doing this most evenings during the summer months when they're not hibernating, and she will be thankful to have one less thing to see to before it gets dark.'

'Come on Fred, let's get going, we've got seven of them to find, and I'm all for making ourselves useful. Great Aunt Alice does so much for us, and besides, she's been battling with terrible toothache. It will be nice for her to know that her beloved tortoises are present and correct before she sets off at the crack of dawn tomorrow.'

'You are good children,' purred Kitton, pleased with himself that he had taken their minds off the perilous journey that lay ahead of them.

It took George and Fred quite a while to find all seven tortoises as they had lots of secret hiding places in the walled garden. George managed to identify each one from the blob of coloured paint on its shell and took photos on her phone to show Great Aunt Alice.

'We've got a surprise slide show for you!' said George, marching into the kitchen. Great Aunt Alice was making a sauce for the spaghetti, but rather than changing into one of her elegant kaftans for the evening, she had decided to indulge herself in the comfort of a luxurious multi-coloured dressing gown that she had been given for her seventieth birthday. She looked wonderful in this somewhat bizarre floor length outfit, accessorising it with an exquisite pearl choker, bracelets and earrings to match.

George took over stirring the sauce, and handed Great Aunt Alice the phone, instructing her to keep pressing the arrow to the right. Sure enough, photographs of all seven tortoises appeared, one after the other. At the best of times, Great Aunt Alice was baffled by technology, but she was enchanted by the children's efforts, and poured herself a large gin and tonic to drink to their health and happiness.

'I adore having you both here and wish you the happiest of holidays at Dar Karmous. Nejwa and Hamdi are joining us for supper so that you can all get to know each other before I leave in the morning. They will sleep in the spare bedroom nearest the kitchen. Fred, could you be a dear and lay the table, they will be here any minute, and I must get on with making the salad. When you've finished that, please listen out for our guests.' Fred jumped to it. He enjoyed being helpful, it made him feel grown up.

Once he had finished his task, he decided to go and wait for Nejwa and Hamdi in the street. They arrived punctually at 7 o'clock, Nejwa dressed in the traditional Djerbian long cream cotton cloak and headscarf, both embroidered with red, black and orange motifs. Like her father, she wore a straw hat on her head. Hamdi held her hand. He was a sweet little boy, four years old, with a mop of curly black hair and enormous brown eyes.

'Hello, my name is Fred. Come and meet my sister Georgina. She is helping Great Aunt Alice with the cooking'.

'Madame Alice has told me all about you both, and it will be lovely for Hamdi and myself to stay with you whilst she is away. Dar Karmous is such a welcoming old house. I often come here to visit Mustapha and bring him eggs laid by my chickens. I've brought some for you as well, so you must let me know how you like them cooked for your breakfast.'

'Wow, what a treat,' said Fred. 'We only get cereal and toast in England – Mum and Dad are always in a rush, and breakfast is a help yourself occasion.' 'Then I shall enjoy spoiling you all the more!' chuckled Nejwa as they strolled across the courtyard. Great Aunt Alice was standing in the kitchen doorway, waiting to welcome them.

'Good evening, Madame Alice. It is very kind of you to invite us to supper. Here are some fresh eggs for the larder. Please may I go into the spare room and quickly unpack the few things Hamdi and I need for our stay? Oh, and you must be George!'

'Yes, that's right, I am so happy to meet you, Nejwa, and just look at Hamdi, he's adorable!'

Soon they were all sitting around the kitchen table, feasting on the dishes that Great Aunt Alice had prepared for them. Everyone was having a lovely time, and the hours flew by. Great Aunt Alice glanced at her watch – it was already 10 o'clock, and she was anxious to get a reasonably early night. Nejwa got to her feet and insisted that Madame went to bed. Great Aunt Alice did not take much persuading. 'Dearest children, I may or may not see you in the morning, depending on whether or not you are awake when I leave. Please make sure you have Nejwa's number tapped into your mobile in case you get into any trouble. I have already given her your number, Georgina.' She kissed George and Fred goodnight, leaving them to help Nejwa with the washing up.

When everything had been put away, George and Fred stepped out into the warm night air. 'What's that loud chirping noise?' asked Fred. 'It's the sound the cicadas make,' replied George. 'They are large insects that look just like overgrown grasshoppers, but it is very hard to actually see them.'

'Well, that's something new I've learnt today, but shush – I think I can hear Kitton sharpening his claws on the trunk of the tall palm tree.' The children stopped in their tracks. Their eyes had adjusted to the darkness, just in time for them to see Kitton clawing his way to the top.

'Crikey,' said George. 'That's Merlin's highest look-out point – easy for Merlin to reach – he has wings, but poor old Kitton, all that way up with only his paws to help him. I think he must be worried that Merlin hasn't returned – maybe something terrible has happened.'

Kitton was exhausted after his steep climb. He made himself as comfortable as he could in the swaying palm fronds, though the constant movement of the tree made him feel really rather queasy. All he longed for now was to hear the gentle flap of Merlin's wings, and to see his feathered friend safely back home.

— Chapter 7 —

Merlin

George and Fred went to bed. There was no point in waiting up any longer. So much had happened in just one day, but they thought if they could get a good night's sleep, they would be up bright and early to kiss Great Aunt Alice goodbye. They were also curious to meet Belgacem, her driver. Great Aunt Alice had told them he lived in Douz, an oasis at the edge of the Sahara Desert. Was this anywhere near Sabria, they wondered? Without giving anything away of their plan to rescue Zeydoun and Lashkar, they would ask him if he knew this village.

'Do you suppose Kitton is having a catnap up there?' said Fred, pleased as punch with his joke. 'Ha ha little brother, you might even make a stand-up comedian one of these days, but right now please shut up. I don't mean to be unkind, but we must save whatever energy we've got for tomorrow. I have a strange feeling that we're going to need all the strength we can muster.' 'Sorry big sister, you're quite right, we must get as much rest as we can, while we can.'

Kitton dozed fitfully. It was past midnight, and he had almost given up any hope of seeing his friend before dawn. But listen! What was that?! Could it be the rhythmic beat of Merlin's wings? He twitched his battered old ears backwards and forwards and gazed hard into the night. Silhouetted against the inky blue sky was the unmistakable shape of a large bird, flying towards Dar Karmous. As it drew nearer, Kitton was able to make out the curve of Merlin's beak. He gave out a joyful miaow, making space for his friend to land safely.

It was hard to know who was the most relieved – Kitton at having Merlin back home, or Merlin at being back home with Kitton. The mission had turned out to be dangerous, taking much longer than expected. 'I'm worn out,' cawed Merlin hoarsely. 'Flying in the dark really takes it out of me. Let's go down to the fig tree, it's much more comfortable than rocking about up here. Once I have had half an hour or so to recover from my ordeal, I will tell you all. But the first thing I am going to do is treat myself to a long cool drink of water from the fountain.'

Just before sunrise, the children were woken by the first of the five daily calls to prayer, a beautiful, haunting sound that wafted from the minaret of the village mosque. It must have been about five o'clock in the morning. Mustapha was already up and about – a devout Muslim, each day of his life began and ended with the reassurance of prayer. George and Fred had been taught to say their own prayers once a day at bedtime, but they often forgot. The church bells back home summoned villagers to prayer usually just once a week, on a Sunday, though if Mustapha's contentment and serenity were anything to go by, then perhaps more prayers and more bell ringing in their village would be better for everyone.

The next sound they were aware of was a soft tap-tap-tapping against the wrought iron bars of their bedroom window. In a nanosecond they realised it was Merlin, trying to attract their attention. 'Good morning George and Fred,' whispered Merlin. 'Please get dressed quickly, and then let Kitton and me into your apartment. It's essential that we talk to you in private. We have a great deal to tell you.'

Early mornings in Djerba are chilly, especially at this unearthly hour. George and Fred would have given anything to spend a little longer in their beds, snuggled up under the cosy camel hair blankets, but they knew there was no time to waste. They clambered into their jeans and jumpers and opened the heavy wooden door into the hallway. Kitton and Merlin crept inside.

'Merlin, there's a bowl of fresh fruit on the table. Shall I peel a banana for you – they're meant to be full of energy and will help to build up your strength. You must be tired out after your exhausting trip.' George didn't wait for him to reply. She peeled the banana, breaking it into bite size pieces for him to pick up with his claws. Merlin was feeling peckish and gobbled up his unexpected breakfast with great gusto. 'And for you Kitton,' said Fred, 'here is a saucer of goat's milk.' 'What thoughtful children,' purred Kitton, licking his lips. Both the banana and the milk disappeared in moments. Merlin and Kitton felt refreshed. Now was the right time to explain to the children the dangers that lay ahead of them. Rescuing Zeydoun and Lashkar was not going to be easy.

George and Fred settled down around the hall table, their pens and journals at the ready. Kitton sat opposite them. Merlin perched on a curtain rail, cleared his throat, and without further ado, and before the rest of the household awoke, began his story:

'Before setting off on my mission, Kitton gave me instructions as to where I would find the Beachcomber Cats: Every evening, they cadge a boat trip to the harbour to join their fisherman friend, Lotfi, who moors his boat there, and can always be relied upon to give them tasty sardines for their supper – the ones that are too tiny for him to sell in the market. In return for his kindness, the cats patrol his hut at night, on the lookout for any rats and mice that might be lurking. An excellent arrangement that suits everyone except for the rodents!

It was scary flying through the flocks of screeching sea gulls who had never seen a bird with exotic feathers before, and for one awful moment I thought they were going to attack me. But somehow I managed to swoop beneath them, flying low along the length of the harbour wall in search of Kitton's friends until, EUREKA, there they were, tucking into their supper aboard Lotfi's boat. They wanted to know who I was, and when I explained I was a friend of Kitton's, they welcomed me with open paws, handing me a slithery silver fish to eat. Trying not to sound too rude, I asked for a drink of fresh water instead. Flying is thirsty work, and between you and me, macaws are rather fussy, only eating fish if it is cooked, and even then, only in tiny amounts. Raw fish is for hardy seabirds, and of course, greedy cats.

Mokhtar was well known to the Beachcomber Cats. They hated him. He had owned many unfortunate camels in the past. He always overworked and underfed them. When they were too weak to carry on working, they were herded off to the market where they huddled together in pens, waiting to be sold for meat. Unlike the other camel owners on the beach who loved their animals, Mokhtar was cruel and uncaring.

He had few friends and was far too mean to build himself a house, or even to rent one. Instead he slept in an old sleeping bag given to him years ago by a French tourist who couldn't be bothered to lug it all the way back to Paris. He had reluctantly shelled out a few dinars in exchange for some grubby blankets that he found on a local market stall and had also invested in a heavy sheet of transparent plastic with which to cover himself and his makeshift bedding when it rained. At night he slept close to his camels in the sand dunes, a safe distance away from the tidal sea water, and where the stunted tamarisk bushes grew. Each camel was tethered to one of these bushes every night with a long rope, but even so, this did not allow them to move about much as their front legs were tied together by a short length of strong cord, a Bedouin tradition known as hobbling, which means that even if the tethering rope broke, it would be impossible for the camel to run away.

All the money that Mokhtar earned from giving the tourists camel rides was spent on cigarettes and beer, which he could buy at the Café Berber across the road behind the beach. It was here that he breakfasted each morning on crusty bread smeared with Jadida butter, accompanied by his other addiction, sweetened mint tea. Each evening, he would return to noisily chew his way through a greasy kebab and a large plateful of lumpy rice. The Café Berber was the centre of his so-called social life which mainly consisted of watching football matches on the widescreen television screwed into the wall, charging his mobile phone, and playing the occasional game of dominoes with a shifty-looking policeman named Ihmed, who was never seen without a pistol tucked into the back pocket of his trousers.

I explained to the Beachcomber Cats how determined you were to return Zeydoun and Lashkar to their kind home in Sabria. The cats' eyes lit up, and they at once gave me directions to the café so that I could see for myself where Mokhtar spends most of his time. In my best parrot French, I squawked 'au revoir' to Lotfi, thanked the cats for their help, and followed my beak across the bay to the beach beyond.

It was getting dark, but my target was unmissable: Each letter of the Café Berber sign was made up of twinkling light bulbs! So this was where Mokhtar hung out! My next task was to find out where Zeydoun and Lashkar were tethered in relation to the café, which even my bird brain told me was far too close for comfort. From the roof of the café, I could see a pebbly track leading down to the beach and reckoned the camels would be somewhere at the other end. Sure enough, in a matter of moments, I landed on Zeydoun's soft fluffy hump.

He turned his majestic head mournfully towards me. He was suffering from blood sucking parasites called ticks, which knowledgeable camel owners remove on a daily basis – but not Mokhtar. You can guess what I did next. I hoovered my way through his furry coat, extracting as many of these nasty insects as I could. Now was the time to whisper the cheering news that you were making a daring plan to return him and his friend to Sabria, and when would be the safest time for this rescue mission to begin. Zeydoun was lost for words. After a minute or two he managed to compose himself 'Between 7.00 pm and 10.00 pm' came his trembling reply, 'and it will take us seven days or so to get there from Djerba, carrying the children on our backs. But how on earth are we going to get off the island without being seen?'

So my dear children, there you have it. You have got many things to think about, but where there is a will there is a way. I have faith that you will find that way, and the people and animals to help you en route.'

George and Fred looked at each other. They would see Great Aunt Alice off, say hello to Belgacem, have a quick breakfast with Nejwa and Hamdi, and then ask Kador to drive them to the harbour as they needed to speak urgently to Lotfi. With Great Aunt Alice away for two days, they must get cracking right away.

'Merlin, what does Lotfi's boat look like?' asked Fred. 'We must speak to him this morning.'

'It is wooden, painted a deep dark blue, with the name Gamara, Arabic for full moon, painted in orange lettering on the stern. By the time you get to the harbour, he will be back from his early morning fishing expedition and will be tidying his nets and floats in readiness for the evening trip. I know he understands French, so getting your story over to him shouldn't be too difficult.'

'Thank you, dearest Merlin', replied Fred. 'You are a clever old bird.'

'Not so much of the old, please,' cackled Merlin jovially. 'Good luck and see you later!'

— Chapter 8 —

Belgacem

Great Aunt Alice was well prepared for her visit to Tunis, dressed in trousers, long sleeved tunic and her most comfortable pair of flat espadrilles. Today, she wore a cotton headscarf topped with a wide brimmed straw hat. Her wrists, as usual, were festooned with gold and silver bracelets, with hooped gypsy style earrings to match. She was never, ever without earrings – she felt positively undressed without them, even though more often than not, they were hidden by whatever sort of scarf arrangement she happened to be wearing.

Not one for elaborate luggage, she had packed what she needed into her two capacious hand-woven baskets, made for her by the sweetest elderly man in the Souk who was famous throughout Tunisia for the objets d'art he crafted out of palm fronds, always working with young supple leaves. He used a unique dye to colour Great Aunt Alice's baskets in her favourite colour, burnt orange.

George and Fred walked over to the kitchen where she was just finishing her breakfast of scrambled eggs, mushrooms and tomatoes that Nejwa had cooked for her.

'Good morning children, how lovely to see you before I go. I have just had a call from Belgacem to say he is five minutes away – perhaps you could go out into the street to welcome him and invite him in for a cup of coffee. He will be tired after his long drive, and I gather he has had to deliver four sheep to a farmer on his way, ones that he has bred himself and can get good money for. His four door Toyota pickup truck comes in useful for all kinds of jobs – one minute he's off loading young sheep and the next collecting a somewhat ancient old lady who wants to be driven to Tunis and back!'

'You're not at all ancient,' exclaimed George. 'I just hope I'm like you when I get to your age – you're such a wonderful mixture of elegance, fun and boundless energy.'

'Thank you, darling George – now please go and wait for Belgacem.'

No sooner had George and Fred stepped into the street, than his vehicle drew up in front of them. Out climbed a smiling man with twinkling black eyes, a hooded brown cloak known as a bernous draped over his shoulders, a pristine white cotton scarf twisted and turned around his head and felt carpet slippers on his feet. He shook hands with the children and was delighted to accept Great Aunt Alice's offer of coffee.

'All things especially good today, Madame Alice, as it makes me very happy to meet your Great Niece and Great Nephew. I do hope they will find time to come and visit me and my family in Douz during their holidays. I would love to show them the Sahara Desert – there are many things for them to see down South.'

'Oh, we'd love to do that,' piped up George, and, without giving anything away, 'are you anywhere near a village called Sabria – I heard from someone I met on the beach that it is a very pretty place, and that only the nomadic Bedouin live there. Fred and I are longing to meet these desert dwellers one day.'

'I know it well and have friends there. It is only half an hour's drive from my house in Douz, where with the help of my sisters, wife, and mother I run a corner shop on the edge of the desert, selling everything from matches to Coca Cola. But business has fallen away. Most of my clients used to be the jolly camel boys who cheerily rode past our shop on their way to and from the camel riding station. Here they would find coach loads of tourists queuing up to ride the ships of the desert, eager to imagine themselves as Lawrence of Arabia for half an hour or so. From dawn until dusk, the boys and their dromedaries turned these imaginings into reality and were proud to show the visitors who came from all over the world the majestic beauty of the sand sea that stretched beyond the verdant green oasis. Tragically, since the Jasmine revolution in January 2011, when the Tunisian people decided they wanted more of a say in running their beloved country, and successfully threw out the dictator who was far more interested in looking after himself than his subjects, what had begun as an era of hope and new-found freedom, was spoilt by the unexpected actions of terrorists whose evil deeds made headlines on the television and in the newspapers. Too many tourists have been frightened away, resulting in hotels having to close down and camel boys having to sell their camels or simply turn them out into the desert to fend for themselves.' Fred and George were looking a bit stunned. 'But enough of this serious talk – we have to believe that things will get better and look at your Great Aunt – she has even chosen to spend her retirement in North Africa, and the people in Erriadh love her!'

'And I love them,' interrupted Great Aunt Alice. 'I could not be happier, apart from my toothache that is, which reminds me, we really must be on our way, we've a long journey ahead of us.' Belgacem carried her two paniers out to his truck, placing them on the back seat. Great Aunt Alice preferred to sit in the front. She bade the children a fond farewell, telling them she'd be back in a couple of days, and not to get into too much mischief in her absence. George and Fred's cheeks flushed uncontrollably, which could have given the game away, but mercifully for everyone concerned the transitional lenses of her purple framed spectacles had turned a dark shade of grey in the early morning sun. She did not have the slightest inkling that something was afoot…

The Toyota disappeared into the distance, and George and Fred returned to the kitchen for breakfast with Nejwa and Hamdi. A mixture of excitement and nervousness made it difficult for them to do justice to the delicious platter of scrambled eggs, tomatoes and mushrooms that Nejwa had saved for them, but George gave Fred a dig in the ribs, indicating that they must eat up, as apart from anything else, this could be their last decent breakfast for days.

Having thanked Nejwa for giving them a great start to the day, they returned to their Haven Apartment and phoned Kador. He said he'd be with them in ten minutes, which gave them enough time to let Kitton and Merlin know that they were off to the harbour to find Lotfi and the Beachcomber Cats, and not to expect them back at Dar Karmous until after lunch.

'I'm going to nip back to the kitchen to tell Nejwa that we should be home at around 3 o'clock,' said George as she stuffed their journals and pens into a plastic bag in readiness to take down vital notes. 'And that sounds like Taxi 431 has arrived – Fred you go and get in, I'll be with you in a minute or two.'

Kador was his usual smiling self, pleased to see the children. He dropped them off at the harbour, saying he looked forward to hearing from them later.

'Gosh George, there are hundreds of boats – how are we ever going to find Lotfi's amongst this lot?'

'Never fear, your big sister is here! If we get completely stuck, we'll ask someone to direct us. These fishermen work in a close-knit community and are bound to know each other'. Sure enough, they were unloading their catch from the night before, shouting loudly at

one another as they compared their hauls. Their faces were weather beaten, their hands as gnarled as the trunk of the old olive tree that grew in Great Aunt Alice's garden. Although the competition was intense, the camaraderie amongst these hardworking men was a pleasure to behold. George's confidence was growing by the second.

'Now then, Fred, we've got to look out for the wooden boat painted in a distinguished deep blue. Most of the ones along here are white, so it shouldn't be too difficult. Because we're early, the fish are still being unloaded, but by the time we locate Lotfi, that job should be finished, and he will have time to talk to us while he's preparing his nets for tonight.'

'Hope you're right,' said Fred.

— Chapter 9 —

Lotfi

The smell of fish was overwhelming. George and Fred were tempted to hold their noses, but that would be impolite, and the last thing they wanted to do was to offend the fishermen. They had almost given up hope of finding Lotfi this morning – maybe he was still out at sea – but wait a moment! Isn't that a dark blue boat moored just inside the harbour entrance? Fred grabbed George's arm. 'There's the boat we're looking for, and the deck has been painted in the same rich burnt orange colour that Great Aunt Alice so loves.'

'A good omen!' exclaimed George. 'All we have to do now is to keep our cool and look for the boat's name.'

To their utter delight, painted on the stern was a curvy line of bold orange lettering, spelling out the word Gamara, plain for all to see! George and Fred were thrilled to bits, though a trifle nervous. They knew they could not afford to fail in getting Lotfi on their side, and that it was up to them to sell their camel rescue story to him. This meant having to remember every word of the French they had learnt at school from Madame Felice.

Lotfi was pre-occupied tinkering with the engine in its box-like compartment at the centre of the vessel. Plucking up courage, George blurted out a shaky, 'Bonjour Monsieur, comment allez-vous?'

'Tres bien, merci, et vous?'

'We're fine,' replied Fred, forgetting to speak in French. George gave him a sharp nudge. Then, to their astonishment, 'Do you both come from England?' enquired the fisherman. The children looked at each other. Were they hearing things, or was this an unexpected miracle? 'Well yes, we do!' answered George. 'We can speak some French rather badly and have picked up the odd word of Arabic. We've only been here three days, staying with our Great Aunt in Erriadh.'

'Welcome to the Port de Plaisance! Meeting you like this is a great way for me to practise the English I learnt as a schoolboy in Houmt Souk. I was told by the teachers that I had an ear for languages, since when I have made a point of talking to foreign tourists whenever the opportunity arises. So what brings you to my boat today?'

'It's a long story,' said George, who was feeling ever so much calmer. 'Then come aboard the good ship Gamara,' beckoned Lotfi, 'and tell me all.' The children stepped down from the quay and on to the stern of the rocking boat, taking care not to get entangled in the piles of fishing nets and floats as they went. They took to Lotfi in an instant. His voice was gentle and his eyes kind. He was a good deal younger than the other fishermen they had so far seen, some of whom had looked rather frightening. Lotfi wiped the engine oil off his hands, sat the children down, and produced three glasses, which he filled with bottled mineral water. Talking was thirsty work, and in case they were hungry, he offered them some dates. He was anxious to put the children at ease, and to make them feel at home, typical of his sweet nature. George did not beat about the bush. 'We need your help. We are desperate to rescue two cruelly treated camels from their horrible owner, Mokhtar.'

'Goodness me, and whereabouts are these camels?' enquired Lotfi. 'Over there,' replied George, pointing to the beach on the other side of the bay. Lotfi looked puzzled: 'But even if you are successful in getting them away from the beach, where are you going to take them? Djerba is a small island where everyone knows everyone.'

'That's the whole point, Lotfi, we have to get them off the island, and onto the mainland. We will then ride them all the way to Sabria, a journey that will take us about seven or eight days,' answered George.

Fred couldn't contain himself any longer. 'Lotfi, would it be possible for you to load the camels onto your boat? Our spies tell us that between 7 o'clock and 10 o'clock at night, Mokhtar is in the Café Berber across the road from where the camels are tethered. While he is eating his supper, slurping beer, and inhaling endless cigarettes, we could untie Zeydoun and Lashkar, and guide them to the good ship Gamara.'

'We don't want to put you under any pressure,' added George 'or indeed get you into any trouble, but if you were prepared to take a risk on behalf of these noble beasts, we would like to put our plan into action immediately – tonight! We realise our mission is fraught with danger, and we completely understand if you don't want to be a part of it. But if you do, we will have to swear you to secrecy right away.'

Lotfi was astonished. The sheer boldness of their plan took his breath away. At that very moment, the Beachcomber Cats leapt onto his boat one by one. George and Fred looked at each other. This was a real stroke of luck, and the timing of their arrival on the scene could not have been better. Not only were they Kitton's friends, but they were also fluent Noah speakers, and the children would be able to tell them about their conversation so far with Lotfi.

'So you've found dear Lotfi and told him of your daring plan? Well, that gets you off to a good start. But has he agreed to join the rescue team?' quizzed Simba, a large broad faced tabby with long grey whiskers and gooseberry coloured eyes.

'No, not yet. He seems to have gone rather silent,' replied Fred. 'That's hardly surprising,' growled Simba, 'but I tell you what, ask him if he would take all of us across the bay in his boat this morning. He can then do a recce of the beach, and from the safety of his boat, see for himself where the camels are, and decide what he wants to do. Don't force him into making a decision – but knowing Lotfi, he will consider your request very carefully.'

Looking Lotfi straight in the eye, George smiled her sweetest smile, and relayed Simba's suggestion to him in English. Lotfi listened. 'There's a lot of sense in that,' pondered Lotfi, all the while scratching his head. But something was troubling him. 'Was it my imagination, or were you and the Beachcomber Cats conversing with each other?'

'Oh I'm so sorry Lotfi – please forgive me! I should have explained, right from the beginning. The cats were speaking to us in Noah, a language exclusive to animals who have studied at The Ark evening classes, and which only children are able to understand. You must think we're mad, but we're not, I promise you. Just a little bit crazy, that's all.'

'Well you can say that again, but as long as it's not me who's going crazy, that's all that matters, particularly at a time like this! Tell Simba I go along with his idea. It will give me time to think things over. There's nothing like being out at sea when it comes to decision making. Whether or not I decide to give you a hand, it is essential for me to work through a great many other factors with you and Fred – what are you going to eat and drink on your journey down to Sabria – how will you find your way, what clothing will you take with you, how are you going to keep warm at night, what will you feed the camels on, where will you find saddle bags large enough to carry everything needed for a hazardous journey of this kind. And remember, there will be nowhere to charge your mobile phone. That reminds me, I will call Papa Ahmid, a wise old Bedouin whose family farms on the mainland, not far from the Port of Zarzis. He has contacts in every village from there to Sabria, people who know the mountain and desert terrains like the back of their hand.'

'Gosh, there's such a lot to take on board,' said George, who although rather pleased with the pun, was beginning to feel apprehensive to say the least. What had she and Fred taken on? There was so much preparation to be done, and so little time left to do it in. Lotfi, with his usual intuition, read her thoughts. 'Come on, let's get going,' he enthused. The cats, who were well used to boat rides and were never sea-sick, arranged themselves on the prow of the boat, ready to direct Lotfi with their furry paws. They longed to see Zeydoun and Lashkar set free just as much as the children did. Lotfi coaxed the engine into life, and away they went.

George found the sea breeze exhilarating. She closed her eyes and turned her face to the sun. For a few moments, she drifted off into a dreamy world of her own. But not for long… 'Please George, I'm not feeling at all well,' groaned Fred. 'I think I'm going to be sick.' He had turned a peculiar shade of pale green. George gently guided his head over the side of the boat, making sure he was facing down wind, so that what remained of his delicious breakfast would be blown away by the wind, and not straight back into his ashen face. Poor old Fred. He just wanted to curl up and die. Just as well, though, to be aware of this unexpected ailment now, rather than later. A quick visit to a pharmacy for some anti sea sickness pills was going to take top priority if the camel rescue plan was to go ahead this evening.

The choppy waves made a swooshing sound as the boat sliced its way through the deep waters towards the seashore ahead. Everyone aboard, especially the Beachcomber Cats on the prow, were doused in salty spray. Getting wet was all part of the exercise, as Lotfi's passengers, two legged and four legged, would soon have to disembark into the shallows. A ridge of rocks jutting out into the sea distracted George from tending to Fred. 'Rocks ahoy,' yelled George. 'I think those are the same ones we saw yesterday.'

'Bravo,' cried Lotfi. 'I will get as close to them as I can without drawing attention to the good ship Gamara. You can paddle ashore, and the cats can swim – they're used to it. I will then take my boat a little way out to sea, and fish with my rod and line for an hour or so. This will give you time to case the joint, and myself time to contemplate the risks involved in your daring rescue plan.'

'Brilliant,' replied George. 'We'll try and locate a secluded spot where the camels can be loaded tonight, and with the help of the cats, I will tell Zeydoun and Lashkar to prepare themselves for the great escape.'

'Aren't you jumping the gun,' moaned Fred. 'Lotfi still has to make up his mind, and if anyone needs rescuing right now, it's me – I'm feeling dreadful.'

'You poor old thing. I promise you will feel better once your feet are on dry land,' commiserated George.

Lotfi found the perfect place to briefly anchor his boat before setting off to do some fishing, having unloaded the children and the cats. This was also to be their meeting point later on in the morning, where they could all report back to each other.

— Chapter 10 —

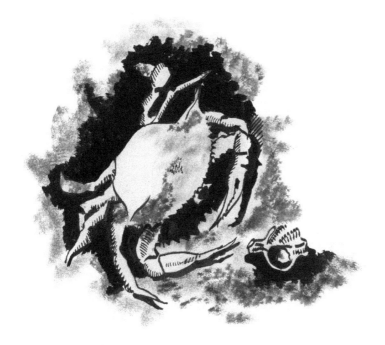

The Beachcomber
Cats

The cats sprang into the sea one by one. They never much liked getting their fur soaking wet, and swimming had never been their favourite sport, but it has its uses. When needs must, as the saying goes, and there was no alternative now but to get on with the job. They felt miffed that a swimming stroke had been named doggy paddle – why not pussy paddle they wondered as they struggled against the tide.

George encouraged Fred out of the boat. They held hands as they waded through the crystal-clear water. 'Ouch!' yelled George. 'I think I've stepped on a sharp stone or something, I'm in agony!' Fred, ever protective of his darling sister, forgot his own troubles in an instant, and peered down into the seabed to search for the cause of her pain. 'There's the culprit,' he shrieked, pointing to a crab scuttling sideways. But within seconds, the crustacean disappeared into its hastily dug sandy hole.

Fortunately, George had remembered to bring the plastic carrier bag with her. As well as putting their journals and pencils into it, she had packed their croc shoes, sunscreen, and a tube of ointment for insect bites and stings. Although a crab could not be classified as an insect, she hoped that by rubbing a dollop of cream onto the claw bite would at least soothe the throbbing and stop the broken skin from getting infected.

The cats were waiting for them, drying their coats in the sun. Simba arched his back and took charge of the situation. 'It's just as well you've had that painful experience this morning. A lesson learnt the hard way. Tonight, you must wear your croc shoes. If we are to get the camels safely loaded onto the boat, complete silence is essential. Shrieks of pain would give the game away, and then we would all be in serious trouble, Lotfi included, though he has yet to give his blessing to this wild venture of yours.'

Just as it had been for Fred, George was distracted from her immediate discomfort. The gravity of Simba's stern voice shocked her. Deep down, though, she had an inkling that Lotfi would not fail them. They did not have to wait that much longer for his decision, and meanwhile they had a hundred and one things to see to.

They were on the same side of the rocks as the Marhaba Hotel. The camels, as the children had discovered yesterday, were on the other side. George lowered her voice and gathered the cats around her under the partial shade of a tamarisk tree. It was vital that she and Fred were not seen with Zeydoun and Lashkar. 'Simba, Fred and I have been thinking – would it be possible for you to be our spokesman, and tell the camels that, fingers and paws crossed, we will be coming for them tonight? And maybe the rest of your canny gang could spread themselves out – some could wander across the road to the Café Berber, and perhaps the others could take a gentle promenade along the beach. We have been taught that cats have a sixth sense and are far cleverer than us humans. Who better than all of you to see how the land lies?'

Simba purred with pride. He was impressed that the children knew about the feline instincts of his species. He agreed to every word they had said, and without a moment's hesitation, ordered his stealthy gang of six to stand to attention before dividing them into two parties of three. He, being the seventh and most senior cat, considered himself the captain. He growled out his orders, commanding them to do exactly as the children had suggested. They were to report back in one hour's time. And now it was left to Simba to scale the jagged rocks, and slither down the other side to where the camels were tethered.

George phoned the Marhaba Hotel, to book a table for an early lunch. She was not the only one making arrangements. Lotfi was doing the same. The children had won his heart, and he did not want to let them down. He admired their courage, but that alone was not going to get them from Djerba to Sabria. They were going to need every bit of help they could get. The solitude of the ocean enabled him to think clearly. He called up his friend Sharif, who earned a living transporting tourists in his horse drawn caleche. Sharif worshipped horses and was inseparable from Bofazer, a chestnut Arab stallion whom he had saved from being turned into sausages by the local butcher.

'Sharif, I am asking a huge favour of you. I have a shopping list of provisions and equipment which I need urgently. I will text you the details. If you are willing to get these things for me, please can you bring them over to the harbour at 4 o'clock this afternoon, when I will be waiting for you on the quayside to unload them onto my boat.

All news when we meet, but please don't say anything to anyone about this.' Sharif, although puzzled, agreed to the challenge. 'Bofazer and I are at your service.'

Lotfi's next call was to Papa Ahmid. They spoke briefly. Papa Ahmid asked Lotfi to call him again if and when they made it to the mainland. He was all for getting these camels back to where they belonged – the desert.

As soon as everyone had done their homework, they met up again. Lotfi had anchored his boat and waded ashore. The children and cats knew from the look on his beaming face that he was on their side. They were thrilled. Now they could put their plan into action.

— Chapter 11 —

The Good
Ship Gamara

The rest of the day sped by in a flash. Darkness descended. George and Fred were quivering with anticipation. They had said their farewells to Kitton and the house, and they were back on the beach, waiting for Lotfi's arrival. Merlin had been grateful for the lift in Kador's taxi – after all, he had a lot of air miles to cover now that the children had given him the daunting role of the escape party's chief lookout officer. He took up his position on the rooftop adjacent to the Café Berber.

The children were crouching in the dunes. Simba was with them. He had ordered his team of six to patrol the road between the café and the beach, having done a recce of the café himself to make sure that Mokhtar was in his usual place, which thankfully he was. The camels were tethered a few yards in front of them, nervously twitching their ears backwards and forwards, their heads held high. They could see and hear things long before their human counterparts. Simba had warned them that morning to prepare themselves for an ocean crossing at nightfall, and now they were on the lookout for the vessel that would sail them away from their miserable existence.

Lashkar heard a faint chug chugging sound in the distance. Zeydoun saw a lantern flickering across the water. The noise grew steadily louder, the light brighter. Both belonged to the Good Ship Gamara. The moment of reckoning had arrived. Lotfi stayed on the boat, while his friend Sharif waded ashore. Lotfi had persuaded Sharif to come along, since he had a natural empathy with animals which would be vital in getting the camels safely loaded onto the boat. They had made a wooden ramp for this purpose, which was lowered into the shallows.

Sharif introduced himself to George and Fred as the newly recruited member of the rescue team.

'You two stay hidden in the dunes while I fetch the camel saddles and carry them to the boat. When I return, we will walk over to the camels in single file, untether them, and lead them single file to where the boat is anchored.' The children's knees turned to jelly. Thank goodness for Sharif's nerves of steel.

Lashkar had broken out into a sweat. He was whippet thin, and the running saddle sores on his bony back provided a constant feast for clusters of flies, even at night-time. He was forever stamping his padded feet in an effort to dislodge them. The idea of clambering onto a boat was an alarming distraction from this irritation. Terror filled every fibre of his being, but lessened with the arrival of Sharif, whose strong hands gave him much needed confidence as he undid the harsh hobbling cord that tied his front legs together. Sharif did the same for Zeydoun, while the children undid the long ropes tethering the camels to the bushes. The short hobbling cords were looped around the camels' necks, and the long ropes attached to the metal rings in their nostrils. The latter arrangement reminded George of Great Aunt Alice's pierced ears. Sharif realised that the children must be given a crash course in camel husbandry before they set off across the mainland. He would see to this later.

Zeydoun was the first to climb the ramp, Sharif whispering words of encouragement in his ear. Lashkar waited nervously for his turn, comforted by George and Fred, their rucksacks slung over their shoulders. Fred had not forgotten to swallow his anti-sea-sickness pills, which made him feel drowsy. A loud thud brought him back to his senses – Zeydoun had made it into the boat's stern. One down, and one to go.

The children handed Lashkar to Sharif. The boat was listing heavily to the port side under Zeydoun's colossal weight. Lotfi needed to get the second camel loaded onto the starboard side immediately in order to correct the imbalance. But the trembling Lashkar refused to budge.

'I tell you what,' said Fred. 'I've got a loaf of bread in my rucksack. I saw Monir rewarding his camels with some yesterday – they gobbled it up. What if I give Lashkar a crust right now, and if he likes it, he'll be keen for more. Instead of a carrot in front of a donkey, it will be dough in front of a dromedary'. Fred, always amused by his own jokes, rummaged into the depths of his rucksack, pulled out the baguette, broke off a piece, and fed it to Lashkar. It went down a treat.

He stepped onto the sloping planks, remains of loaf in hand. Lashkar followed, Sharif at his head, George bringing up the rear, gently tapping Lashkar's hind quarters with a stick that she had picked up on the beach. It was not unlike loading reluctant ponies into a trailer.

After what seemed ages, everyone was on board and no bones had been broken. Sharif commanded Zeydoun and Lashkar to couch down, their angular legs folded underneath them, their long necks outstretched on the decking. Lotfi hauled the ramp and anchor back onto the boat. Breathing a sigh of relief, he took the helm. They were on their way at last.

George snuggled up to Zeydoun, Fred to Lashkar. The cosiest way to keep warm. The camels found the motion of the boat unsettling, but the children's presence was reassuring.

So far, so good thought Simba to himself. The camels are seaborne. I must get word to my gang. We have to prepare ourselves for Mokhtar's reaction when he returns from the café to find that his animals have vanished. He'll be confused after a long session of swilling beer and smoking cigarettes, but to confuse him further, there will be no tell-tale footprints in the sand to give away the escape route, as the cats will have swept these away with their tails.

The cunning Beachcomber Cats completed their task swiftly and silently under Simba's supervision. Job done, they hid behind a pile of driftwood and waited. A swooshing of wings heralded Merlin's arrival. Stifling a squawk, he landed in their midst. 'Mokhtar is on his way.'

— Chapter 12 —

Shocks
All Round

Great Aunt Alice's grandfather clock struck on the hour every hour. Hamdi was fascinated by this gigantic toy, counting the chimes on his fingers. Shrieking with delight, he ran towards his mother, all ten fingers held high in the air. Nejwa did not need reminding how late it was. She was beside herself with worry. Great Aunt Alice had phoned in at teatime to say she had arrived in Tunis, and that she and George had spoken on their mobiles. Nejwa had been trying to get through to George all evening, but without success. She did however manage to get hold of Kador, who thought it strange the children hadn't pre-booked their return taxi ride to Dar Karmous. He remarked that they had been unusually quiet on their ride down to the beach, and for some reason or other, unbeknown to him, they had brought Merlin the Macaw with them.

Nejwa dragged two mattresses into the kitchen. From this room, which was directly opposite George and Fred's apartment on the other side of the courtyard, she would be able to see and hear any comings and goings. She flung the French windows wide open and snuffed out the candles. Hamdi flopped down onto his makeshift bed, fully clothed, clutching his beloved teddy bear. He was out like a light. Nejwa propped herself up into a sitting position with plump cushions from Great Aunt Alice's drawing room. She knew that sleep would be impossible, but she could at least put her feet up.

Hamdi stirred – was that purring in his ear, or was he dreaming? He opened his eyes to see a cat stretched out beside his teddy. 'Shoosh Hamdi, it's only me, Kitton. I've some important news for you to pass on to Nejwa.' Kitton was whispering in Noah. He had spent many an hour teaching Hamdi this unique language that only animals and children are able to understand. Hamdi was his star pupil, and all those hours of lessons and homework were now going to prove invaluable.

'George and Fred are not coming home tonight. They have embarked on a dangerous mission to return two maltreated camels they befriended on the beach, back to their desert home in Sabria. This will take at least a week. Merlin has agreed to accompany them. He will fly back to Dar Karmous from time to time with progress reports.'

At that very moment Merlin was winging his way from Café Berber to report to Simba that Mokhtar was belching his way back to the beach, his belly full of beer. As is customary with the hard drinkers in Djerba, he orders two bottles at a time of the local Celtia brew, knocking back at least six bottles an hour. Simba stood under the tamarisk bush, his back arched into a capital D, bracing himself for Mokhtar's return. He intuitively sensed tension in the air. The bush rustled. Merlin had landed. 'He'll be here in a matter of minutes,' he squawked. 'We must make ourselves scarce – quick – there's a pile of driftwood over there, the perfect hiding place from which we will be able to see and hear everything'.

Sure enough, Mokhtar staggered into view, a cigarette dangling limply from his tobacco-stained lips. A shock awaited him – his camels were nowhere to be seen. He searched in vain for their footprints in the sand, but there were none, and their long ropes had vanished. Blind with rage and disbelief, he shouted for his policeman friend Ihmed at the top of his voice. But Ihmed was out of earshot. There was nothing for it but to make his way back to the café, even though he was in no fit state to do so.

As luck would have it, he found Ihmed in the road just about to go home on his motor bike, his leather belt and holster slung round his waist, pistol at the ready. Ihmed was sober. His profession did not allow him to drink on duty, although as far as he was concerned, he was never off duty – there was nothing he liked better than showing off his firearm. Mokhtar was in a drunken stupor, waving his arms wildly in the air. 'What on earth has happened?' questioned Ihmed.

'My camels have gone. I need your help.' Ihmed's eyes lit up at the prospect of a chase. There was nothing he liked better than catching people and locking them up in a cell. With some difficulty, he hoisted Mokhtar onto the pillion seat of his motorbike. Their first stop would be the scene of the disappearance – the beach.

Simba and Merlin had stayed put. The Beachcomber Cats were hiding under an upturned wooden boat nearby, in readiness for any instructions that Simba might give them. Simba's ears flattened at the sound of an engine whirring towards them. Then there was silence. The motorbike came to a standstill, within feet of the driftwood pile. He recognised Ihmed's harsh voice at once – this man had a reputation for kicking animals that got in his way, and was even known to have purposely run over cats, leaving them to die at the side of the road.

He was a cruel man, probably why he and Mokhtar got on so well – it takes one to know one. Not so long ago, Simba's gang had composed a cats' chorus dedicated to Ihmed. 'We want Ihmed dead. He's killed our feline friends. But what goes round comes round. Be sure of our revenge.'

To the utter dismay of these two vile men, there were no clues as to who or what might have gone off with the camels – not even a give-away footprint. The Beachcomber Cats stifled their purrs of delight. They were thrilled to have bamboozled the policeman by sweeping away any tell-tale traces with their furry tails. Ihmed was furious. He didn't like being made to look a fool. He was mystified. Clearly the camels hadn't just wandered off, as their saddles, cords and ropes had been taken. The only item left behind was a sack of mouldy old grain. 'It must have been thieves,' he muttered to himself as he pulled his mobile from his pocket. 'The first thing I must do is to call my colleagues at the Ajim Ferry police station, alerting them that two camels have gone missing – one black, the other white. I will ask them to search each truck before it crosses over to the mainland. Whoever has taken these animals will want to get them off the island of Djerba where everyone knows everyone and news travels fast. It would be almost impossible to sell on a black and a white camel, even to the hard-hearted butchers for meat. My second call will be to the marine police who have a vessel that patrols the island's coastline twenty-four hours a day.'

Merlin, who had an ear for languages, including Noah, took all of this in, his head cocked to one side. He had listened to all kinds of conversations in Great Aunt Alice's kitchen, learning many of the phrases off by heart. He and Simba exchanged knowing glances – they must stay put until they saw what the next move was.

'Mokhtar, you will have to come with me to my police station in Midoun, perhaps even spending the night there. We have to make an official report of this incident, which I will circulate to every policeman and soldier patrolling the island. You wait, we will have the culprits locked up in no time.' And away they went, the bike's front headlight glaring into the darkness of the night.

Simba and Merlin came out of hiding and went to tell the Beachcomber Cats they could do the same. A plan had to be made, and fast. 'Merlin, you fly to the good ship Gamara to warn George and Fred what is happening, and they can pass this on to Lotfi. Stay with them until they have landed on the mainland, and until you have found out what the next phase of their journey is. Then fly back to Dar Karmous and speak to your friends there, before setting off again with the children and the camels in the direction of the desert. It is going to be an exhausting few days for you, and you'll need every ounce of energy you possess. I am going to cadge a lift back to the harbour on one of the night fishermen's boats, taking my gang with me. I don't want the police to get wind of the part we have played in this extraordinary escape. I bid you an affectionate farewell and safe journey. Try and get word to me from time to time through your network of feathered messengers and I can give them messages from this end to pass back to you.'

— Chapter 13 —

Land
Ahoy!

Sharif was busy changing the colour of Zeydoun's and Lashkar's coats. Zeydoun was now pale grey, Sharif having mixed together a concoction of wood ash and grey dye. Lashkar's white coat had turned into a shade of chestnut by dying it with henna, a substance used by the Bedouin women to paint intricate coppery patterns on their hands, feet, sometimes even their faces. The distinctive brand marks on the camels' hindquarters and cheeks were not going to be so easy to disguise, but fortunately they had not yet shed all of their winter fur, which kept their identities hidden. The good ship Gamara rocked gently from side to side, a motion similar to riding a camel. Lotfi was looking at his marine charts by torchlight; his aim was to find Lunar cove on the mainland, suggested by Papa Ahmid as the ideal secluded spot for the landing. Here there were no steep cliffs, but instead olive groves that rolled down to the seashore. Better still, it was Papa Ahmid who owned and farmed this land. Lotfi breathed a deep sigh of relief – there in red letters were the two magic words he had been searching for: Lunar Bay.

Gamara's prow dipped in and out of the waves as she headed towards her destination. George and Fred soothed the camels, whilst Sharif explained to the children that he would accompany them ashore with all the kit they needed for the long journey ahead of them. There was rather a lot of it, and he wondered if George and Fred had any idea of what they had taken on. But Papa Ahmid had come up with a helpful plan during his earlier phone conversation with Lotfi. Just as a baton is passed on from runner to runner in a relay race, he would arrange for the escape party to be passed on from shepherd to shepherd from the moment they disembarked until the moment they arrived in Sabria. Flocks of sheep and goats were to be found in all the different terrains en route – in the cultivated olive groves, in the hills, in the mountains and in the plains rolling down to the desert itself. Papa Ahmid knew the land like the back of his wrinkled hand, just has he knew the shepherds and their Bedouin families who tended the herds.

Fred felt something sharp dig into his shoulder. 'Don't move Fred,' whispered George. 'It's Merlin. I think he has something to tell us.' Merlin cleared his throat and asked for some water. He was thirsty. 'The bad news is that Mokhtar is with Ihmed the policeman. Every

police station in Djerba has been alerted to look out for two stolen camels, and the marine police are patrolling the island's coastline with their boat which is equipped with powerful long-ranging laser beams. The good news is that they have no idea that you have already left the island – they think you are heading overland to the ferry at Ajim, where the police have been ordered to check every truck crossing over to the mainland. You have got off to a flying start.' George passed these tidings on to Lotfi, whilst Merlin ruffled his feathers, chuffed at the adjective he had chosen.

Adnene the shepherd boy snuggled into the warmth of his bernous – the cloak that his grandmother had woven for him out of camel, goat and sheep wool. His grandfather, better known as Papa Ahmid, had sent him down to Lunar Cove for the night to look out for Lotfi and his unusual cargo. Like most shepherds, Adnene never went anywhere without his flute – it was his constant companion. He loved the haunting melodies he played every bit as much as he loved the deep silence of the countryside, which was only broken by the rise and fall of the wind and the bleats of the sheep and goats. For the next few hours, silence ruled. Each and every one of his senses was tuned in to the boat's arrival.

Lotfi had a deadline to meet: to get the camels onto dry land before dawn broke. 'Land ahoy,' whispered Sharif into the skipper's ear. 'Don't speak to soon,' replied Lotfi. 'My charts show there are hazards ahead.' Sharif did not need to question this statement any further. There was an almighty thump. The good ship Gamara juddered to a halt and was listing heavily to portside at an alarming angle. 'Just as I had feared,' groaned Lotfi. 'We've run aground. This sandbank will keep us captive until the tide comes in. Sharif, please take the children to starboard. We need to get as much weight on to that side of the boat. The camels must remain where they are – couched in the centre.' Fred explained the situation to the camels with as much confidence as he could muster. They were frothing at the mouth with fear, and if the truth be known, Fred's tummy was churning. 'We're not going to sink are we?' he stammered. Sharif, who had visions of all his hard work dying the camels' coats being washed away, and worse, could only reply, 'Hopefully not, Inshallah.' Time was running out, and the tide needed to come in fast if they were to get Zeydoun and Lashkar ashore under the cover of darkness.

Adnene shifted his lookout spot onto a high dune. The tide was coming in at the rate of knots. Dawn was breaking. What was that noise? Adnene's heart missed a beat – it sounded like a sputtering engine. He cupped his hands over his eyes and gazed out to sea. The object of his all-night vigil was drifting in his direction. He stripped off his warm clothing down to his underwear, took a deep breath, and swam to the good ship Gamara. To everyone's relief, and thanks to the tide changing in the nick of time, Lotfi's boat was afloat once more. 'Hey George, look over there. There's someone swimming towards us.' Lotfi too had spotted this welcome sight. Although his navigating skills had failed to avoid the sandbank, he had at least found Lunar Cove.

Adnene was strong – swimming against the tide did not faze him. Hours spent herding sheep and goats every day accounted for his fitness which he also put to good use in his village's junior football team. Fred leant over the side of the boat, ready to give Adnene a helping hand. Within minutes he was safely aboard. He spoke softly in Arabic to Lotfi and Sharif, pointing to where the vessel should be beached, and the camels unloaded.

Sharif had already made up his mind that he would accompany the escape party as far as Papa Ahmid's farmhouse. He would spend the morning giving George and Fred a crash course in saddling and unsaddling, loading and unloading Zeydoun and Lashkar, as well as demonstrating how to hobble them and tie them up at night. The children would have to make do with the most meagre of diets, as every inch of room in the cavernous saddle bags was needed for the sacks of grain to feed the dromedaries. George and Fred would have to survive on what used to be the traditional diet of the Bedouin: Dates, khobse (unleavened bread) which the shepherd boys had been taught to make and bake, and fresh goats' milk. The most precious commodity of all though, for both man and beast to survive, was water from the wells – without it, the party would perish. Local knowledge is beyond price. The success of this daring escapade depended upon it.

— Chapter 14 —

A Shock for
Great Aunt Alice

Merlin presided over the beaching of the boat. The camels stumbled down the ramp behind Sharif, with George and Fred bringing up the rear. The sun had risen. There was not a moment to spare. Papa Ahmid's house was one hour's camel ride away through the shady olive groves. Sharif's expertise came into its own. In no time at all, his charges were ready to take the first step of their journey, George on Zeydoun, and Freddie on Lashkar. Adnene walked beside Zeydoun, leading the way. Sharif kept a few paces between himself and Lashkar, so that he could observe how the children were managing with their riding, and if the balance of the baggage was to his satisfaction. Merlin would not begin his homeward journey back to Dar Karmous until he had seen them all disappear into the distance.

Lotfi was preparing to go out to sea – he checked the boat for any damage. Thankfully, it was unscathed. He filled up the petrol tank and oiled the engine, which had to be put into reverse to get Gamara off the beach. At last, she was back where she belonged, bobbing on the ocean.

Merlin perched contentedly on the prow. Lotfi was pleased to give him a lift for part of the way. Merlin knew he had to save up his strength for the miles of flying that lay ahead. A boat ride was the ideal start to his day. When he took off next, it would be for his flight to Dar Karmous, to update Kitton and Hamdi on the events of the past few hours.

Several hundred miles away to the north, Great Aunt Alice was indulging herself in a slap-up buffet breakfast at the Hotel Africa in Tunis. Although she actually stayed in a much smaller, less expensive family run hotel around the corner, because she had recommended so many of her friends to the Hotel Africa, it was the management's way of saying thank you for the business she had brought them. Yes, she felt very spoilt, but the staff reminded her that she deserved to be! She delved into the depths of her basket in search of her mobile. Her dental appointment was not until 12 noon. Strong pain killers had made a good night's sleep possible, and more this morning meant that she made the most of the sumptuous breakfast. She would not need any lunch.

'Good morning, dear Nejwa, how are you, and how are George and Fred – behaving themselves, I hope?'

Nejwa had been dreading this call. How was she going to explain what Hamdi had told her. She took a deep breath: 'Madame Alice, the children are not here. They are on a seven-day journey down south to Sabria.'

'What?' exclaimed Great Aunt Alice, wondering if the medication she had taken had caused her to hallucinate. Surely she was hearing things?

'No, I'm afraid it is a fact. They have taken it upon themselves to liberate two cruelly treated dromedaries they found on the beach and return them to their original owner in the Sahara.'

'How do you know all this?' retorted an astounded Great Aunt Alice.

'Through Hamdi, who has the gift of conversing in Noah, a unique language only understood by children and animals – that is if they have attended Noah evening classes. Kitton spoke to him earlier this morning. Merlin will be the flying messenger, returning to Dar Karmous with regular progress reports.'

'Nejwa, has the sun got to you, or have you gone completely off your rocker? I have never heard such a ludicrous tale.'

'Neither of those things, Madame Alice, I am speaking the truth.' Great Aunt Alice beckoned the waiter. She needed the strongest cup of coffee he could lay his hands on.

Merlin landed softly on the kitchen table. Kitton jumped up beside him. Hamdi was wide-eyed with excitement. Both he and Kitton were agog as to what Merlin had to say next. Nejwa looked on helplessly. No doubt Hamdi would fill her in and it would be her unenviable task to call Great Aunt Alice with the latest news.

— Chapter 15 —

Sharif

The children took their lesson on camel handling seriously. They knew their lives depended upon it. A slipping saddle or a leaking jerry can could spell disaster, or even death. They risked their necks if they fell off, and their very existence if the water supply ran out. They also had to tend to the needs of Zeydoun and Lashkar – if one of them became sick, they would be in real trouble. Sharif had given them ointment to treat Lashkar's sores, and shown them how to remove blood-sucking ticks if Merlin wasn't around.

George and Fred had kept their personal belongings to a minimum, most of which they had stuffed into their rucksacks hitched to the front of their saddles. Sharif had packed two second-hand sleeping bags into the main baggage, plus a large folded sheet of plastic which would come in useful if it rained. The heaviest items were the sacks of grain for the camels, the sacks of flour for the bread making, and the bulky branches of dates.

Papa Ahmid filled the jerry cans with water from his well, whilst Sharif showed the children how to tie the traditional Bedouin scarf, known as a chech, around the head, neck and shoulders. Every precaution has to be taken to prevent sunstroke, including wearing long loose cotton trousers and long-sleeved loose cotton shirts which George and Fred were already wearing. They carried matches in their pockets for lighting fires, and Fred felt especially important to be the one carrying the Swiss Army penknife that he had been given for his birthday.

Sharif was confident. The time had come for George and Fred to continue their overland journey. He wished them luck and bade them a fond farewell. They waved him a tearful goodbye, both rather wishing he could have gone with them. They had grown fond of this sweet, kind man in the short time they had known him. Now they had to go it alone, but not completely...for there in front of them was the sturdy Adnene, quietly leading the camel train on foot. It was comforting for George and Fred to realise that from hereon there would always be a shepherd boy to guide them to their journey's end.

Sharif hitchhiked his way to El Jorf, the small mainland port operating regular ferry crossings to the Isle of Djerba. He had phoned his brother, Tarek, asking if he and Bofazer could please meet him outside the Café Etoile in Ajim, the ferry port on the Djerbian side of the water.

He stepped off the flat-bottomed boat and began his ten-minute walk to the café. He was looking forward to being reunited with his horse-drawn caleche and pleased to be on home territory once more.

His contemplative thoughts were shattered all too quickly. A shouting match was going on inside the police station which he was passing. Mokhtar, having spent all night in Ihmed's Midoun police station, had insisted he be taken to speak to the police in Ajim, who informed him that in spite of checking every single truck and lorry, sheep and goats were the only livestock they had come across. There were no camels. Mokhtar went berserk, even turning on his so-called friend Ihmed, grabbing him by the scruff of his neck. 'I'll get my camels back no matter what it takes, and I'll make whoever took them pay.' The fierce exchange of words was so loud that it was abundantly clear to Sharif who these two desperate characters were. With his tongue in his cheek, he walked on by.

— Chapter 16 —

A
Dilemma

As he was driving along in his truck, Belgacem's mobile rang. It was Great Aunt Alice. 'Good morning, Alice, all things good?'

'Well not exactly, my dear Belgacem. I have a crisis on my hands, the reason for which I will explain when I see you. I must fly down to Djerba this afternoon. A second night in Tunis is out of the question.'

Belgacem parked his pickup truck outside the dental surgery. Great Aunt Alice emerged, nursing her mouth with a large bloody cotton handkerchief. 'He had to take the tooth out. An unpleasant ordeal involving three lots of anaesthetic which will take a while to wear off, but at least the extraction has been a distraction from the alarming conversation I had with Nejwa this morning.'

Great Aunt Alice regaled the story to Belgacem in muffled tones as he drove her to Tunis Carthage Airport for her 15.45 flight. 'I need to ask a big favour of you, Belgacem. Once you have dropped me off, would you be prepared to drive on to Djerba and stay tonight with me at Dar Karmous? I know it would be nicer for you to get back to your own family, but I really could do with your help and advice, not to mention moral support.'

'I am at your service, chere Alice. Always.'

'Thank you, Belgacem. I am hugely grateful.'

Great Aunt Alice checked in for the hour-long flight, travelling light with just one of her baskets, which counted as hand luggage. This would save time when she got to Djerba Airport. The rest of her stuff was safely with Belgacem in his truck. Before boarding, she rang Kador, asking him to meet her and drive her directly to the harbour. She had gleaned yet more unlikely details from Nejwa during their second conversation that morning, the gist of which was that a fisherman by the name of Lotfi had assisted George and Fred in their bold plan to save two camels from their brutal owner.

Great Aunt Alice climbed into the front passenger seat of Taxi 431, the dependable Kador holding the door open for her. She decided against filling him in on what had happened, but took in what he had to say about dropping the children off at this very same spot yesterday morning. She asked him to please wait for her here until she had finished her business, and then head for home. It did not take her long to find Lotfi and his boat. She introduced herself to him, and listened to his tale, stunned and moved by what she heard.

He had risked his livelihood, and Sharif's too, in agreeing to George and Fred's request – in the eyes of the law, both men could be found guilty of aiding and abetting a crime. The law would not consider the children's actions as a deed of compassion, the view held by Lotfi and Great Aunt Alice, but as outright theft.

'I could not refuse George and Fred. Their innocent determination bowled me over. Through my contacts I have been able to put a workable plan in place for their mission to succeed – not without its dangers, I grant you, but they have made an excellent start. Sharif and myself are sworn to secrecy, and the same must go for Nejwa and Hamdi. Mokhtar will stop at nothing to find his camels, but it is my belief that at the moment, he thinks they are still on the island – long may that misconception last.'

Great Aunt Alice was pleased to be back at Dar Karmous. She felt more in command of the situation now that she was in the familiar surroundings of her own home. She asked Nejwa to prepare a chicken couscous for supper, which would keep nicely for Belgacem to tuck into later after his long drive. He could sleep in George and Fred's apartment. But right now, a hot bath beckoned. She scooped a large handful of ginger scented bath mousse into the running water, lit a jasmine scented candle, and immersed herself into the tub, but not before she had gargled with a saline solution specially prepared by the dentist, and taken the first of the antibiotics he had recommended. Although her mouth was sore, the excruciating pain had vanished, along with the rogue tooth.

Feeling refreshed and revived, Great Aunt Alice dressed in her brightest kaftan with accessories to match. She did not wear a headscarf this evening, as she wanted her silver blonde hair to dry naturally, having treated it to a thorough shampooing and conditioning.

She walked through to the kitchen and over to the fridge. She was in need of a large glass of chilled wine with her supper and opted for a bottle of white 'Jour et Nuit', having made sure before leaving Tunis that her dentist had not prescribed antibiotics that prevented her from drinking alcohol. Nejwa was thankful that Madame Alice had returned to the fold and had not accused her of negligence. 'Nejwa, my dear, please don't feel in the least bit guilty at what has happened. When Belgacem arrives, we will have a discussion as to what to do next.'

A bottle of wine later, Alice heard a knock on the courtyard door. It was Belgacem. Mustapha let him in, and escorted him to the kitchen. 'Good evening, ma chere Madame Alice, how are you tonight – looking much more relaxed than you were in Tunis, me thinks.'

'I feel it,' she replied, unable to conceal her delight at welcoming her dear friend to dine at her table. 'Let me pour you a Coca Cola, but first Nejwa will take you over to George and Fred's apartment so that you can wash before supper.'

Belgacem and Great Aunt Alice had a soft spot and mutual respect for each other. He was a devout family man with a beautiful Bedouin wife and four adorable children. She was a free spirit who by choice had never married, preferring to pursue her career, content to enjoy her sister's children and grandchildren. This did not mean she was without admirers – there had been plenty. Belgacem applauded her courage to up sticks and retire to a foreign country. He felt so proud that she had chosen his country, Tunisia.

They sat long into the night at the kitchen table. A second bottle of 'Jour et Nuit' had been opened. This did not offend Belgacem, whose Muslim religion didn't permit alcohol of any kind. Although Great Aunt Alice relished a glass of wine and the occasional gin and tonic, he had never seen her the worse for wear, and she always had the grace to ask him first if he minded her having a drink, which in English speak amounts to an alcoholic beverage! And he never did mind.

'Belgacem, I am faced with a dilemma – whether or not to ring the children's parents. One half of me says yes, the other no.' Belgacem retreated into one of his long silences, which Great Aunt Alice was used to. After what seemed an eternity, he came back with his answer. 'Settle for no. Let us call them once their mission has been accomplished. If they were entirely on their own, it would be different. But from what you have told me, they will be accompanied. Papa Ahmid, one of the most revered members of the Bedouin, and whom I have known since the days when he owned a large herd of camels near Douz, has obviously given his blessing to the children's courage.'

And on that upbeat note, they bade each other a very good night and peaceful sleeping.

— Chapter 17 —

The
Storm

Sitting high up on Zeydoun's back, and looking down at the red soil far below, George's imagination went into overdrive. What if I hit my head on a tree, what if I fall off, what if Zeydoun spooks at something? It had only just dawned upon her what a ginormous animal he was. She felt like the proverbial pea on a drum. Fred was much closer to the ground on the pathetically thin Lashkar. Papa Ahmid had shown him how to treat the oozing saddle sores with the ointment that Sharif had bought. It made Lashkar roar with pain – the stinging sensation was almost too much for the poor camel to bear, but Fred quoted the 'no pain, no gain' phrase, promising his emaciated friend that these agonising injuries would soon be a thing of the past.

It was late afternoon. The camel train padded silently along, Adnene walking bare foot in front, turning around from time to time, making sure the children were secure in their saddles. He stayed as close to the olive trees as possible, avoiding the open ground in between the groves where they could be spotted. But they were still on Papa Ahmid's land, so there was no immediate threat – well at least from prying eyes.

'How are you doing Fred?' ventured his sister. 'Okay George, but I've just felt big drops of rain. I hate getting wet. Do you think we should get the kagools out of our rucksacks?' 'I don't think it's much, little brother, let's just wait and see.'

Adnene could smell the rain – he had been brought up to do that. Sure enough, within half an hour, the sky was pitch black. George was quick on the uptake this time. 'Adnene, please tell the camels to stop while we put on our kagools – we can do this without having to get off.' Thank goodness George has spoken up said Fred to himself. She might have thought I was being feeble if I'd asked him. No sooner had the children pulled the waterproofs over their heads than the heavens opened. Thunder rumbled in the distance. In a matter of moments, the camels were up to their fetlocks in red mud as the ground around them turned into a quagmire, a footing they were not used to. All of a sudden, forked lightening lit up the darkness, making Fred jump.

Adnene reacted quickly. He knew the danger they were in. Metal was a lethal conductor of lightning, and there were George and Fred, clinging to the slippery iron handles on their camel saddles. He was desperate to find safe shelter for them all. He knew they weren't far away from one of his overnight stops – a hut made from hurdles of plaited palm fronds with a thick thatched roof. He urged the camels to walk faster. Fred began to cry. The downpour had turned into a full-blown electric storm.

When they got to the hut, the camels were reluctant to lower themselves into the quagmire. Adnene had to tap them sharply on their shoulders to make them obey his verbal commands. George and Fred dismounted, exhausted. It had been a long ride, covering a lot of ground. Their arms and legs were aching. They were damp too, and as the evening closed in, their teeth began to chatter with the cold. Adnene did his best. In no time at all, he had everything neatly stacked in the hut, and Zeydoun and Lashkar tethered to bushes well away from the olive trees which could be struck by lightning. It was still pouring down and far too wet to light a fire, but from his own canvas bag he pulled out his bernous and a warm wool blanket for the children to huddle under. He handed round dry biscuits and a tin mug of goat's milk for their supper.

George and Fred took off their wet trainers, already dreading the thought of having to put them on again in the morning. Fortunately, the contents of their rucksacks had remained reasonably dry. They got out their torches and rummaged around for their Ice Breaker Merino wool sweaters.

Adnene hung his outer clothes to drip dry from wooden pegs in the corner of the hut, and George and Fred did the same with their kagools. 'What if we want to go to the loo in the night, George?' 'Just don't think about it,' she answered. 'We were given time to look after that before we got caught in the storm, and that will have to last us until the rain stops.'

Adnene's acute sense of awareness once again came to the rescue. To soothe the children's nerves, he played them a tune on his flute. This had the added advantage of lulling them into a fitful sleep. He too was in need of rest – another long day lay ahead of them.

George and Fred were awakened by a loud clap of thunder directly overhead, followed almost immediately by the sound of branches crashing to the ground. Adnene was already on his feet. He told the children to stay exactly where they were while he went outside in the rain to see to the camels. 'I'm not going to pretend to be brave any longer,' blurted Fred. 'Neither am I, darling brother. Let's just admit it. All we can do is look after each other. What will Great Aunt Alice have to say when she finds out that we have left Dar Karmous?'

'She will be cross, very cross. I wonder if she has told Mum and Dad that we have gone missing? If so, they will be worried witless.'

'Yes' said George. 'They will catch the next available flight to Djerba, and order a missing persons search, which will put the whole of our camel rescue plan in jeopardy. On the other hand, Great Aunt Alice is not a drama queen. She is as passionate as we are against cruelty to animals – you only have to look at those seven rescued tortoises living happily in her garden. I have a feeling deep down that she will be on our side.' 'Oh, I do hope so, George. We'll keep our fingers and toes crossed.'

Adnene checked that Zeydoun and Lashkar had come to no harm. Mercifully, they had not shifted from their tethering place, and although wide-eyed with fear, they had not met with the same fate as the olive tree, whose branches had been shattered to smithereens by a bolt of lightning.

The bedraggled Adnene returned to the hut for what remained of the night. Despite the roof creaking worryingly under the weight of the rainwater, the children had dropped off to sleep again.

When George woke in the morning, without thinking, she threw her arms around Fred. Warm sunshine streamed through the open door. Adnene had been up and about since 6 o'clock, gathering wood and getting a good fire going. He looked forward to baking bread in the ash and lit a second fire, which they could all sit around for breakfast. George and Fred were none the worse for their rough old night. Adnene had put their trainers out to dry by the fire, so they put on their second pair of shoes – flip flops – and went outside to join him.

What they saw next stopped them in their tracks: Fred and George looked at each other. They were both reeling with shock. George was the first to speak 'I can't believe it Fred. Last night's storm has washed away the dye on Zeydoun's and Lashkar's coats – what are we going to do? – they have gone back to their original colours.'

'Well, we could start by smearing them in red soil – their legs and tummies are already covered in it.' Fred felt protective of his beloved sister and pleased with his practical idea. George rewarded his initiative by giving him an affectionate pat on the back. 'Well done, little brother. I'm impressed. Let's get to work immediately.'

The camels revelled in the attention. They were perking up. Adnene had given them the feed they had missed out on last night, and they felt the warmth of the sun caressing their backs.

— Chapter 18 —

The Painting
Class

The Dar Karmous household was up bright and early. Mustapha was as usual the first one to rise, followed by Nejwa and Hamdi. Mustapha had promised to walk his grandson to nursery school after breakfast, which would leave his daughter free to attend to the household chores. At Great Aunt Alice's request, Nejwa and Hamdi were to stay with her for as long as it took George, Fred and their guides to get the camels safely to Sabria. Belgacem had emphasised the importance of having Hamdi around – he was after all the Noah interpreter, and the only one able to translate messages from Merlin and Kitton.

To Hamdi's delight, today's lesson was painting – his favourite! Senna the art teacher told the children to paint something that made them feel happy. Hamdi filled a jam jar with water, into which he dipped his paint brush before opening up his box of paints. The morning passed far too quickly for him. He was having such a lovely time. Two matchstick camels could be now be seen striding across his sheet of paper, one ridden by a matchstick girl, the other by a matchstick boy, both wearing what looked like straw hats. A huge yellow sun shone out of a cloudless blue sky. Hamdi was a thoughtful little boy – to complete the scene, he decided to paint some green palm trees and a silvery pool of water for when his subjects got too hot and needed to quench their thirst in the shade. He was proud of his efforts, and so was Senna. The fat boy sitting next to Hamdi took a closer look at his neighbour's jolly picture, and then burst into uncontrollable tears, cross that his one of a policeman on a motorbike hadn't caught Senna's attention.

Great Aunt Alice sat at the head of the table, pleased that she had talked Belgacem into staying on for lunch. Nejwa had made a mouth-watering salad of new potatoes, prawns, hard boiled eggs and chives, beautifully presented in a bed of crisp green lettuce. Great Aunt Alice cut the warm baguette into chunky slices, and asked Belgacem to help himself to her home-made lemonade before pouring out a glass for herself and Nejwa.

Hamdi came rushing into the kitchen in a fever of excitement, waving his painting in the air. 'Look, Mama, the teacher has given me a gold star! I was best in the class today. We were asked to do a picture of what made us happy. Look what I did!' He unfurled the sheet of paper, laying it out flat on the far end of the kitchen table. The grown-ups put down their knives and forks and went over to inspect it. A deathly silence descended in the room. No one spoke for what seemed like ages.

'What's the matter, don't you like it?' blurted Hamdi. Great Aunt Alice was the first to speak.

'Well done, darling. Your painting is wonderful, but who else has seen it, other than Senna?' 'Only the fat boy who sat next to me. He was crying because I got the gold star, and he didn't.' 'And what was his painting of?' asked an ashen-faced Nejwa. 'Of a policeman on a motor bike,' came the reply.

Great Aunt Alice and Belgacem looked at one another. Hamdi, through the innocent eyes of a child, had, without meaning to, given away a vital clue – George and Fred's compassion for camels – which, if it got into the wrong hands, could be disastrous.

'Well, it's no good crying over spilt milk. We are where we are,' said Great Aunt Alice in a matter-of-fact manner. 'The cat may or may not be out of the bag, and we stand a fairish chance that it isn't. In either case, the children have our utmost support, and we will not let them down.'

Hamdi's lower lip trembled. Belgacem put a comforting arm around him and then around Nejwa, who was feeling physically sick.

'I think we should all sit ourselves down and have something to eat,' commanded Great Aunt Alice reckoning that this was an appropriate moment to pour herself something a little stronger than a soft drink. As she went to open the fridge door, Merlin flew into the room, landing onto the bowl of oranges, his midnight blue feathers in dazzling contrast to the fruit. He could not have timed his entrance better.

Hamdi's eyes lit up – for whatever he had mistakenly done wrong, here was his chance to make amends. He sat bolt upright, ready to interpret the latest report on the children's progress.

— Chapter 19 —

The
Salugi

George and Fred had given Zeydoun and Lashkar new disguises, Zeydoun wearing a coat of strawberry roan, and Lashkar one of terracotta. The red soil had worked wonders.

Adnene's aim today was to reach the mountain foothills for their overnight stop. Here he would hand over his responsibilities to his colleague, Khalifa. However, between the comparative safety of the olive groves and the distant undulating hills, they would have to ride across an open patchwork of small farms growing vegetables, flowers, crops and vines. Adnene knew most of the farmers in this area, as well as the many footpaths that criss-crossed their land. He was confident that no eyebrows would be raised or questions asked as he passed through with George and Fred. But crossing the main road beyond was not going to be a walkover – wouldn't it be easy if it was just that?

George and Fred relaxed into the morning ride. They were warm, dry and happy. Tempted as they were to sing along with the birds soaring above, Adnene stressed that they must keep quiet. This reminded George of her Mum quoting the phrase 'children should be seen and not heard'. George tinkered with the words in her head, coming up with her own version 'children *and camels* should *not* be seen *or* heard.' Not until they got to Sabria, that is. Meanwhile, they must do everything in their power to keep out of sight and out of earshot.

Their brief lunch stop was under a clump of young eucalyptus trees, close to the farming community. Donkeys and mules, some pulling carts, were the only form of farm machinery and transport. This was not the place to light a fire. Adnene handed round the extra loaf he had baked early that morning. He was getting twitchy about negotiating the main highway, and how he was going to avoid the soldiers carrying out routine road checks.

George and Fred thrived on Adnene's bread, and shared pieces of it with Zeydoun and Lashkar when Adnene wasn't looking. The camels had forgotten what it was like to be rewarded. They were pathetically grateful and would try their very hardest to give the children a comfortable afternoon ride.

The hum of traffic grew louder as the main road drew closer. From Zeydoun's great height, George was able to make out a stationary queue of trucks that had been flagged down into a layby. She passed this information on to Adnene, who brought the camels to an abrupt halt. Somehow, he had to find out what was going on before they took one step further, but how? 'What's up?' asked an anxious Fred. His question went unanswered. All eyes were transfixed on a large cream coloured dog racing towards them.

Within minutes, the panting animal flopped down at Zeydoun's feet. It was a Salugi, the elegant breed of racing hound prized by the Bedouin for its hunting skills and speed in the desert. Zeydoun felt a sudden pang of homesickness for the Sahara. And then something unexpected happened… 'My dear friends, you are in grave danger'. George and Fred could not believe their ears. The Salugi spoke Noah.

'Adnene, please ask the camels to get down for us – me and Fred must get off and go and listen to what our Salugi friend has to say. I will translate into French for you.'

What the Salugi told them sent a shiver down George's spine. Fred began to shake from head to toe: Posters offering a reward for the capture of Zeydoun, Lashkar and their thieves, believed to be a boy and a girl, had been slapped up all over Djerba, and beyond to the mainland. At the foot of the posters were the words: 'Theft is a crime. The punishment is a heavy fine or a prison sentence.'

What George had seen from the vantage point of Zeydoun's tall back was a police stop and search operation. Adnene had to think fast. George had passed on the Salugi's message to him. Zeydoun and Lashkar were confident the noble hunting hound would not betray them. He was from aristocratic desert lineage, and the camels in their wisdom had sworn him to secrecy.

The Salugi made a cautious return to the layby via a deeply dug ditch. He did not want anyone to see where he had come from. In one graceful leap, he landed in the back of his master's truck, and curled up with the sheep his master had recently purchased in Tatouine market.

After the police had satisfied themselves that there were no camels hiding in amongst the sheep, they allowed the vehicle to continue its homeward journey to Douz. Dromedaries are never to be seen standing upright in pickup trucks. Instead, they fold their long limbs under their tummies, and crouch on the floor, couch being the correct Arab term for this sedentary position.

Adnene had to get as far away from the stop and search scene as possible. The heat of the day was both enemy and friend – enemy because it made walking twice as hard, and friend because it lulled the police into having a break for a cigarette and even a snooze…

He encouraged George and Fred to keep going. Normally, they would all be resting when the heat was so intense, but at least everyone else in the locality was. The coast was clear for him to continue. He made use of a tree-lined track, making sure they could not be seen from the road which ran parallel to the route he had chosen. On and on they walked. But Adnene knew what he was doing. They would rest up a bit when the sun went down, and cross the highway when darkness fell.

The sun was sinking over the horizon – a welcome sight for the children's sore eyes. Tired out, they were longing to get off the camels. Adnene handed them dates to munch during their break. Their legs and arms still aching, the moment came for them to climb back on to their mounts. It was dark as they made their way towards the road. The camels were startled by the headlights of a passing lorry. Adnene took his time and a deep breath. All was quiet. It was now or never. Over they went. But there were many more miles to leave behind them before their rendezvous with Khalifa. The flat ground leading to the foothills offered no hiding places for potential prisoners. But there was no need to worry – the night was their guardian angel.

— Chapter 20 —

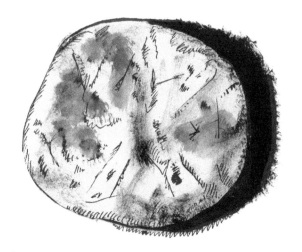

Goat
Stew

Riding in the dark was a novel experience for George and Fred. The inky blue sky was studded with stars, from which Adnene took his bearings. His knowledge of the constellations stood him in good stead. Within three hours, they should be with Khalifa. No more walking bare footed from now on; the ground was stony, and he had put on his carpet slippers, the unlikely form of footwear favoured by the Bedouin.

George began to feel faint with tiredness, flopping about like a rag doll. Fred too was done in, but didn't want to let on to his sister. Adnene glanced over his shoulder and gave the children a gentle reminder to remain alert. A small lapse in concentration could have dire consequences. George pulled herself together, correcting her deportment. It was worth the effort! Was that a fire she saw burning in the far distance? Could it be where Adnene was aiming for? Would the magical moment arrive when they could finally get off their camels and rest their aching bones?

'Listen George – I can hear music – it sounds a bit like my recorder back home.' 'Yes, you're right Fred. I think it's someone playing a flute.' The camels too responded to the sound, twitching their ears backwards and forwards. They were every bit as keen to rest their legs and longed for their evening feed. It was 9 o'clock, way past their supper time.

The haunting notes of the flute drew nearer. They had arrived at Khalifa's camp! George and Fred had to be lifted off their camels. Their arms and legs could barely function. Adnene removed the saddles as quickly as he could and arranged them around the campfire for George and Fred to lean against. Khalifa introduced himself to the children. He handed them coarse woollen blankets to sit on, and a mug of goat's milk to share, before going to help his friend. George and Fred warmed their hands over the fire. What bliss! They were curious to find out what was cooking in the cauldron which sat firmly on a metal tripod above the flames.

They didn't have to wait long. As soon as Adnene and Khalifa had finished tending to Zeydoun and Lashkar, they returned to the campfire. The hospitable Khalifa had prepared a goat stew for his weary guests. Adnene's eyes lit up. There was nothing he liked better than chewing meat straight off the bone. Khalifa removed the cauldron lid with a flourish, gave the stew a good old stir, and doled out steaming helpings on to three tin plates. 'Yuk,' grimaced Fred. 'I won't eat goat meat.' 'Be thankful for what you are about to receive,' reprimanded George. 'You sound as though you are saying grace,' retorted Fred. 'It's not so much that, dear Fred, simply that somehow or other I have to make you realise this will probably be the last hot meal you will get for the next few days, so just be grateful for what you are being given.' Fred drifted into a minor sulk. George pinched him hard. 'Okay bossy sister, but what are we going to eat it with – there are no knives, forks or spoons.' 'With your fingers, silly. Just like our host – and he's even baked bread for us to mop up the sauce with.'

It was almost midnight before George and Fred turned in. They wriggled deep down into their sleeping bags, which Khalifa had placed a safe distance away from the dying embers of the fire. They rested their heads on the soft pillows that he had improvised from sheepskins, and gazed awestruck at the heavens until they couldn't keep their eyes open any longer. They were spending their very first night under the stars.

The shepherd boys talked quietly amongst themselves long into the early hours. Shepherding is a lonely existence, and the chance to share local gossip with a kindred spirit is irresistible.

— Chapter 21 —

Wake Up
Call

B efore putting a plan into place, Merlin had consulted his crow friends, the Corbeaux brothers, Café and Chocolat. These glossy feathered birds, famed for their orienteering skills, always knew the shortest flight paths to take, hence the saying 'as the crow flies'. Café and Chocolat explained the lie of the land as clearly as they could, all the way from Papa Ahmid's farm right down to the village of Sabria and were able to advise where the shepherds usually graze their flocks. Merlin listened carefully.

For the first leg of his journey however, Merlin had taken up Belgacem's kind offer of a lift in the Toyota pickup truck. He reckoned on getting as close to Khalifa's camp as possible before the sun went down, roosting overnight in a tree, and taking off at first light the next day in search of the escape party. Unlike the nocturnal owls, he hated flying at night. Belgacem dropped him off just before the stop and search layby en route to Douz.

Merlin was not the only one up at the crack of dawn. Khalifa was already gathering wood for the fire, and Adnene had gone to see to the camels. George and Fred were still fast asleep, but not for much longer! 'Time to get up, time to get up,' squawked Merlin in his best English accent. 'Rise and shine, rise and shine.'

The children wriggled out of their sleeping bags, grumpy at being so rudely awakened. It took them a minute or two before they realised where their wake-up call had come from – goodness gracious, it was Merlin! How wonderful! All traces of grumpiness vanished.

After the initial excitement of Merlin's arrival, the mood changed. Over breakfast, the serious subject of crossing the mountains was raised. Khalifa said it would take three or four days to get to the other side with the camels, but probably only one day's fast walking for him to retrace his footsteps back to camp. It was arranged that Adnene would look after Khalifa's flock until his safe return. Merlin was happy to find the children and camels in good spirits – so far, so good. George thought it would be a nice idea to scribble a note to Great Aunt Alice, which Merlin could courier back to Dar Karmous.

The camels loaded, the farewells said, the next task was to give the dromedaries a long drink at the well nearby, and to fill the jerry cans with water. George and Fred decided to walk on foot until Zeydoun and Lashkar had quenched their thirst – it would be sensible to stretch their legs whilst the going was good. Up until now, they hadn't really taken in the precipitous peaks that soared above them, but in broad daylight it became horribly obvious what they had to tackle. 'I'm not sure I'm up to this,' whispered George. 'I know,' said Fred, 'I feel a bit the same, but at least we can comfort ourselves that Ihmed and Mokhtar won't be able to get anywhere near us up here.' 'That's true,' replied George. 'This landscape is made for gazelles, not men on motorbikes.'

'George, Fred – can you please hold onto your camels whilst I heave the water out of the well and pour it into that trough – don't let them go until I tell you to'. The camels were longing for their drink, and started to stamp their feet. Fred tried to soothe Lashkar, telling him to be patient. The very thought of liquid refreshment prompted Lashkar that it was time for a pee, and Zeydoun followed suit...

'It's okay for them to have their drink now,' announced Khalifa. Zeydoun and Lashkar did not hesitate. They lowered their handsome heads into the sparkling fresh water, slurping it down with great gusto. Such a pleasant change from all that salty stuff Mokhtar used to give them! Their flanks expanded visibly as they took their fill. Khalifa allowed them to take their time. It would be a while before they reached the next well.

— Chapter 22 —

Vertigo

The mountain pass writhed and slithered around the boulders in snake-like fashion. To begin with, the climb was gradual. The U-bends were a manageable distance apart, the ground underfoot reasonably smooth. George regained her confidence, and Fred was becoming almost blasé about the challenges that mountaineering on camels presented – it was the ultimate cool as far as he was concerned, far more impressive than rock climbing. Nobody in his school would ever believe the story he had to tell when he re-joined his class for the summer term. He must remember to take some photographs as proof.

Then there was the fun of camping in caves at night, the camels acting as watchdogs, alert to the slightest sound, whilst Khalifa and the children slept. These were precious hours for Zeydoun and Lashkar, who ruminated about the happenings of the day. Khalifa had given them extra quantities of grain for their evening feed, as there was very little vegetation for them to eat at this altitude. Their padded feet were sore, but the kindly Khalifa examined each pad every evening, removing any foreign objects that might cause pain. Walking along mountain passes was not something the camels found easy, but it was a case of chew the cud and bear it – if it wasn't for the bravery of the children, whom they were growing more and more attached to with each passing day, they would still be in the clutches of the cruel Mokhtar.

On the morning of day three, the terrain changed dramatically: The U bends came thick and fast, the slopes were scarily steep, and the valley below had disappeared from sight. The dromedaries negotiated the narrowing footpath with trepidation, leaving the rock face to their left, and the sheer drop to their right. Khalifa walked ahead at a steady pace. He knew and loved the mountains, but had to admit that crossing them with camels and children in tow made him just a tad nervous.

As for George, her confidence had been overtaken by fear. There was nothing between her and a drop of thousands of feet below. Suffering from vertigo, she was on the literal edge of disaster, riding one of the tallest camels in existence along a path more suited to the cloven hooves of goats.

And then it happened. A landslide of loose stones hurtled down the rock face, startling Zeydoun who, in his effort to avoid them, lurched violently. Both his right legs, front and hind, dangled perilously over the path's edge. George screamed. Fred shouted.

Khalifa reacted: 'Your penknife, please Fred, as quick as you can.' Within seconds, Khalifa cut the rope attaching Lashkar to Zeydoun. One camel in trouble was bad enough. Two would be catastrophic. As so often happens in the mountains and in the desert, extra help seems to appear from nowhere in an emergency. Walking towards them was an old man leading a donkey. He sized up the situation in a glance. Not a word needed to be exchanged. The two men worked as one. George was lifted to the ground, a blanket wrapped around her shaking body. The old man calmed Zeydoun in softly spoken Arabic whilst Khalifa gently eased his dangling legs back onto the path. The immediate crisis over, Fred asked if he could get off Lashkar so that he could go and comfort his sister.

'It's no good, Fred. I can't go on. Watch out, I think I'm going to be sick.'

'You'll feel loads better if you are,' encouraged Fred, remembering what their mum used to say to them on such occasions back home. But it wasn't as simple as that. Waves of nausea swept over George, but try as she might, nothing happened. She attempted to stand, but couldn't. Everything within sight was spinning round and round. 'I'm feeling so dizzy, Fred, I just want to lie down and die'. 'Please don't say that, George, you're going to be okay. I am here to look after you.' George curled up into a tight ball. Fred told her to stay put, which in retrospect he thought was a daft remark, as it was horribly obvious that right now nothing on God's earth would make George move one single inch from where she lay. She had drifted into a deep sleep.

The old man and Khalifa made a decision. Khalifa would walk slowly on with the dromedaries as far as the midday stop, and the old man, whose name was Salah, would stay with George, Fred and the donkey until such time as George felt strong enough to continue. Zeydoun broke out into a lather of sweat. He too didn't know if he could go on, but both he and Lashkar realised they were at the point of no return – how did the saying go? 'Between a rock and a hard place'? Well that sure summed up how they felt about these hostile mountains – boulders on one side, a bottomless chasm on the other. But the thought of life back with Mokhtar was all they needed to spur them on towards the distant sweet sands of Sabria.

After about an hour, Salah made a fire with some small twigs.

He pulled a blue enamel teapot out of his canvas bag, together with a brown paper bag filled with dried camomile flowers, and a jar of honey. By means of sign language (he spoke very little French) he indicated to Fred that he was going to brew camomile tea flavoured with honey, a well-known herbal remedy for curing tummy troubles and anxiety. The crackling flames caused George to stir. Very slowly, she sat up, too frightened to open her eyes. Fred put his arms around her. 'Salah is brewing camomile tea for you, which he promises will make you feel better.'

Salah handed Fred a tiny tumbler of warm scented tea for him to give to his sister. 'Take a sip of this, George.' Fred held the glass to her lips. George began to drink. Whatever it was tasted good thought George, but where am I, what has happened?

'Try and drink some more,' coaxed Fred. Salah's potion was working its magic. George opened her eyes to find her world had stopped spinning. By the time she had finished the third glass, the nausea had all but disappeared, but the events of the morning came flooding back.

'Where's Khalifa?' she asked, 'and where are the camels?'

'They've gone on ahead to where we'll be stopping for lunch,' replied Fred.

'Fred, I don't know how to tell you this, but I am not getting back on to Zeydoun.'

— Chapter 23 —

Phone
Calls

Great Aunt Alice's iPhone rang. The caller's name flashed across the screen. It was Sarah, her niece. She took a deep breath. 'Good evening, Sarah, how are you my dear, and how is Russell?'

'We're fine, but more importantly, how are you? I do hope George and Fred aren't wearing you out. Children can be so exhausting, especially if you aren't used to them.' Great Aunt Alice needed to keep her wits about her. Another deep breath was necessary.

'They're such fun to have around, and have taken to Tunisia like ducks to water. They're not here at the moment, as they've gone off on a supervised desert excursion for a few days which involves camping and camel riding. They begged me to arrange this for them, and I am afraid I gave in.' Great Aunt Alice hoped the good Lord above would forgive her for telling a white lie. She felt He would understand that there's a time and a place when white lies come in useful.

'Gosh! Lucky things! You spoil them, Great Aunt Alice!'

'It gives me nothing but pleasure, dearest Sarah. They'll phone you when they're back at Dar Karmous – the signal in the areas where they are travelling is virtually non-existent, so don't expect to hear from them.'

Great Aunt Alice heaved a sigh of relief when the conversation with Sarah came to an end. She had got away with it. Rewarding herself with a large gin and tonic, she put a call through to Belgacem.

'Good morning Madame Alice. How are you? Everything alright?'

'To be perfectly honest Belgacem, I'm not quite sure. Merlin made it safely to the mountains and back, bringing with him a scribbled note from George assuring me that she and Fred are fine, though a shade twitchy about negotiating the rocky passes. That doesn't worry me nearly as much as the sight of all those posters dotted about the place offering a reward for the return of the camels. No good beating about the bush Belgacem - in the eyes of the law, Zeydoun and Lashkar have been stolen, and although it has yet to be proved, you and I know that George and Fred are the thieves.'

'Madame Alice, you are forgetting that George and Fred are on a mission of mercy, liberating two animals that have been subjected to cruelty and starvation. Why, I've even heard that in some countries, there are charitable organisations that rescue cruelly treated beasts of burden, often paying good money for them. Sadly, some of these poor animals are beyond saving, and have to be put to sleep. You never know, the law might look favourably upon George and Fred, but let's not cross any bridges until we get to them – they have yet to be caught.'

'Whatever the outcome, Belgacem, I have already set cash aside to pay for the camels. I must get to Sabria as quickly as I can. Rumour has it that Ihmed is making his way down to the Sahara on his motorbike, with Mokhtar riding pillion. Are you free to come and collect me from Dar Karmous later on this afternoon?'

'Madame Alice, I am at your service.'

Great Aunt Alice packed. Hamdi spoke with Merlin and Kitton. It was decided that Merlin would accompany Great Aunt Alice to Sabria – Belgacem's truck being the perfect take-off and landing pad for Merlin's desert forays, saving him hours of flying time. Great Aunt Alice made a quick recce of George and Fred's apartment to check if there was anything of theirs they might be glad of when she finally caught up with them. She bundled some clean T-shirts, shorts and underwear into her basket. It wasn't until she was just about to leave the apartment that she noticed Georgina's yellow camera sitting on the wooden chest in the hallway. 'I'd better take this as well,' she thought.

Hamdi would have loved the ride down to the desert, but Great Aunt Alice knew this would have subjected the little boy to intense questioning at the checkpoints. Merlin was sorry to lose his interpreter, but the flying courier system he and George had put into practice worked well. Air Mail in its purest form.

— Chapter 24 —

Donkey
Ride

For the first time in his life, Fred understood the meaning of responsibility. His sister was a bundle of nerves after her frightening experience, and although the camomile tea had steadied her, she was still not strong enough to walk. There was only one thing for it. To persuade George to ride Salah's donkey. By now, Fred was an expert in sign language. Wise old Salah responded.

'George, the donkey will carry you to our lunch stop. Salah will lead him, with me walking alongside you on the path's edge. Just pretend you are playing Mary in the school nativity play, and that I'm Joseph.' She did not have the strength to argue with her brother. Salah lifted her into the saddle and commanded his donkey to walk on.

By the time they got to the cave, Fred and Salah had found a solution to George's fear of riding Zeydoun in the mountains. Salah had agreed with Fred not to leave them until they reached the rolling plains leading to the Sahara – George riding the donkey, Fred riding Lashkar, and Khalifa riding high on Zeydoun. Fred asked Salah if he could get this over to Khalifa, while he would take it upon himself to brief the camels. The last thing either Fred or George wanted was to hurt Zeydoun's feelings. He was an armchair of a ride, the most comfortable camel in the world, but too tall for George in these vertiginous surroundings. The second grown-up lesson that Fred had learnt today was the art of tact.

Khalifa and the camels were happy with Salah and Fred's plan of action. The donkey and camel train, led by Salah, negotiated the remainder of the mountainous route without incident, the caves providing shelter from the sun at midday, and from the wind at night. George and Fred loved curling up in the caves after supper, with the couched camels just a few feet away from where they slept. Washing in freezing cold mountain streams was not quite so cosy, and had taken a bit of facing up to, but better that than feeling filthy dirty.

With a mixture of relief and sadness, the day came for them to make the final descent to the rolling plains below. The mystery of the majestic mountains had cast its spell over the children. George had established a close bond with her donkey, whose sure-footedness had banished her fears of falling, and Fred had promoted himself to sibling in charge. Both children had risen to the challenges of the past few days. An overwhelming sense of achievement swept over them.

Khalifa's final duty before handing over his responsibilities was to give the camels a long drink of water, and to replenish the almost empty jerry cans. It was at the well a mile or so ahead where he intended to meet up with Adel, the shepherd boy who would guide George and Fred to their ultimate destination: Sabria.

'I am going to miss dear old Salah and his sweet donkey,' piped up George. 'Me too,' said Fred. 'I don't think we could have made it without them, and Khalifa has been a real star.'

You could hardly see the well for the sheep and goats jostling for a drinking place at the water troughs. Watering holes are the gossip centres of the wilderness, where nomads congregate to exchange news in excited, high pitched voices. Khalifa had difficulty picking out Adel amidst the throng of people and animals. It was George that spotted him first.

Salah's donkey was familiar with this well. He made a beeline for his favourite trough, George still in the saddle. She was determined not to get off him until the very last minute, dreading the moment when she had to part with her trusty steed. He pushed his way through the bleating herds and lowered his head into the water, his long ears twitching contentedly backwards and forwards. George patted his shoulder, her eyes welling up with tears.

'Why are you so sad?' came a voice from the melee of shepherds and livestock. George pulled herself together. Standing beside her was a boy with the most beautiful face she had ever seen. A white chech framed his exquisite features, his dark oiled skin glistening in the morning sun. For a moment, she was lost for words, realising that whatever ones came into her head would have to be in French.

'It's just that I will soon have to say goodbye to Khalifa, Salah and his very dear donkey. They have become such steadfast friends. But at least we don't have to part with the camels.'

'Who's we?' enquired the shepherd boy 'And by the way, my name is Adel. What is yours?' George could not believe her ears.

'I'm Georgina,' she stammered. 'I'm with my brother Fred, who's over there with Khalifa, Zeydoun and Lashkar.'

'Just the news I have been waiting for. When your donkey and my goats have finished drinking, we will go and join them. Khalifa has told me all about you.' Adel held out his hand 'I am happy to meet you, Georgina.'

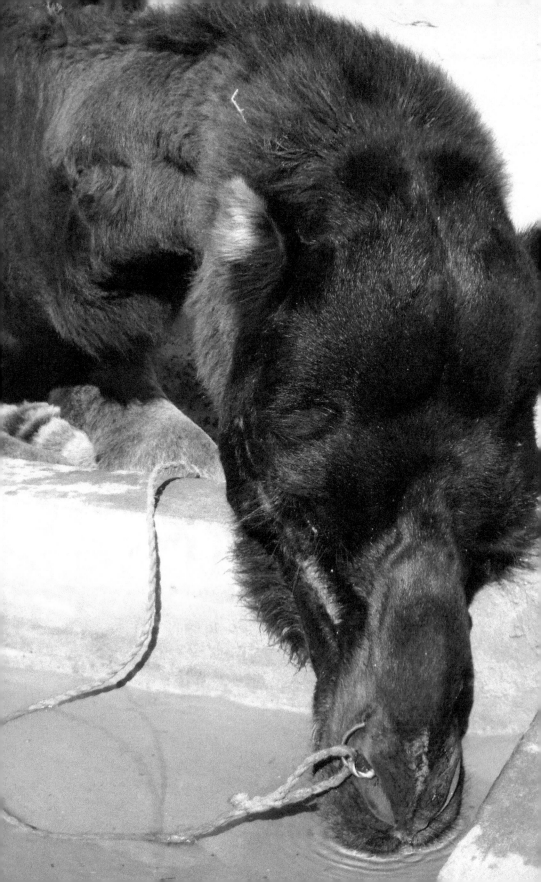

The dromedaries had quenched their thirst. Khalifa had filled the jerry cans in readiness for the handover to Adel who was now walking towards him followed by George astride her beloved donkey.

'Good morning, Adel – how are you, and how is your family? Everyone in good health, I hope.' Adel responded in the affirmative, before asking Khalifa exactly the same set of questions. This traditional exchange of affectionate greetings is never hurried, involving handshakes, manly hugs, and a kiss on each cheek. 'I see you've already introduced yourself to George. Let me introduce you to her brother, Fred, and to the camels Zeydoun and Lashkar'. Khalifa was going to miss his charges, but handing over the responsibility for them was a mammoth weight off his shoulders. He had fulfilled his role, as had Adnene. Now it was Adel's turn, assisted by his frolicking herd of goats. There would be no shortage of milk to drink, and Adel had stocked up on dates as well as flour for the ritual bread making.

Khalifa led the camels to a quiet spot. Riding Zeydoun had been an unexpected pleasure. He hoped so much to see him again one day. He stroked the dromedary's roman nose and looked into his wistful brown eyes. 'Thank you for carrying me safely, Zeydoun.' And he thanked Lashkar too for taking care of Fred.

The time had arrived for the party to re-group. Khalifa couched the camels. George handed her donkey to Salah, unable to speak. Fred and his new-found knowledge of sign language came to the rescue. With a series of gestures, he was able to express his and his sister's profound gratitude to Salah. The old man was moved.

The children climbed on to their camels. Khalifa blew them kisses, Salah waved, the donkey brayed, and away went the trio, back from whence they came.

— Chapter 25 —

Roadside
Encounter

Mokhtar and Ihmed were on the point of falling out big time. The 'Reward' posters distributed by the police had failed miserably. Nobody had come forward. Mokhtar was convinced his camels were no longer on the Isle of Djerba and demanded that he and Ihmed should conduct a search of their own. Ihmed agreed – they would ride his motorbike as far as the oasis town of Douz, famed for its camels and cameleers.

Forty-eight hours had passed since Mokhtar had held a bottle of beer to his tobacco stained lips. None of the little cafés on the mainland sold alcohol. Being denied access to his daily fix made him more aggressive than ever. Ihmed did not know how much longer he could take his passenger's insults. They had ridden up, over and down the mountain highway, and were now speeding along an inviting stretch of level road. If Mokhtar doesn't show a little more respect, Ihmed thought to himself, this is where I shall tell him to get lost. From here on, he can find his own way into the desert. I shall simply do a U-turn, and head homewards.

Just as Ihmed was warming to the prospect of having the motorbike to himself, he jammed on the brakes, bringing the bike to a sudden halt. A mule drawn cart was crossing the otherwise empty road, the pitiful animal cringing under a hail of whip lashes, struggling to pull an impossibly heavy load of bricks. It takes one cruel owner to recognise another. Mokhtar and the mule driver hit it off in an instant.

'I've never owned a mule,' shouted Mokhtar. 'But I did own two riding camels – that is until they were stolen from me.'

'Funny you should say that,' yelled the man with the mule. 'I saw a couple of camels only yesterday. You'll never believe me when I tell you they were being ridden by children, yes children, and foreign ones at that from what I could see.'

Ihmed switched off the running engine and propped the bike up against a milestone. At long last they were on to something. Mokhtar pulled a packet of cigarettes from his pocket and handed them around. 'What colour were these camels?' he demanded. 'The smaller one was a reddish colour, and the larger one greyish red,' replied the man with the mule. Mokhtar's face fell, but he was not going to give up. 'Tell me more about the children – were they boys or girls? And by the way, what is your name?' 'One of each, and my name is Fawzi, what is yours?'

Names were exchanged, followed by the inevitable formal greetings. Fawzi is the Arabic word for triumph, and what a triumph this roadside meeting was turning out to be for Mokhtar and Ihmed. But for George and Fred, the seeds of a potential disaster had been sown.

It was too much of a coincidence – Fawzi's description matched the naïve painting that Ihmed's fat son had seen in the art class at Erriadh. Yes, the colours of the camels differed, but Ihmed reckoned there could be reasons for this – not only was he an official policeman, but he also considered himself an unofficial detective.

Fawzi pointed in the direction of the well. It was at least a couple of miles or so from where they stood. Ihmed feared for his motorbike. Was it going to withstand the rigours of the cross-country tracks ahead? But there could be no going back now. Ihmed and Mokhtar clambered on to the machine. Their blood was up. Both men were hell-bent on cornering their quarry.

— Chapter 26 —

The
Sandstorm

Great Aunt Alice ensconced herself in Belgacem's house where she was graciously received by his entire family: Aisha his wife, and their four children; his brother and sisters, nephews and nieces, and most important of all, his mother, the revered matriarch around whom the whole household revolved.

'My home is your home, Madame Alice. You are my guest. You are most welcome to stay here as long as it takes the children to get Zeydoun and Lashkar safely to Sabria. Even longer if you like.'

'Thank you Belgacem. But for your kindness I would be a nervous wreck. Never in my wildest dreams did I envisage seeing the Sahara under such bizarre circumstances. I wonder how long we will have to wait before our feathered courier returns with the latest message from George and Fred.'

Merlin had taken full advantage of being chauffeured. Travelling at speed in a vertical sitting position, rather than his usual horizontal flying one, was such luxury. Settled comfortably on the back of Great Aunt Alice's car seat, he allowed his wings to relax, and took in the passing scenery at his leisure.

Belgacem's children were beside themselves with excitement at having a macaw to stay. Worried that he might get lost amongst the acres of date palms outside their back yard, they decided it would be sensible to take their exotic new friend on a little tour of the oasis so that he could get his bearings. The children fought amongst themselves as to whose shoulder he should perch on, but Merlin, ever the diplomat, suggested they take it in turns. Happily, everyone understood... thankfully, everyone spoke Noah!

It was of course vital for Merlin to get his bearings at sky level as well as ground level before nightfall. The children were quick on the uptake, realising it would soon be dark. Merlin swooshed skywards whilst the four chattering youngsters hopped and skipped their way home.

On Merlin's second lap of the oasis, he was confronted by a couple of territorial crows. Merlin was the first to speak. 'Are you by any chance related to the Corbeaux brothers, Café and Chocolat?' he enquired, hoping that a bit of familiarity would break down any hostility. 'Why, yes,' they cawed in unison. 'We're cousins, but what brings you down here, all the way from Djerba?' 'It's always been an ambition of mine to converse with the migrating birds in the Sahara,' squawked Merlin, keeping all his claws crossed that this unlikely answer would satisfy them. It did. His inquisitors allowed him to pass. Merlin returned to Belgacem's courtyard, where the children greeted him with handfuls of seeds and chopped fruit. He spent the night on the roof of Great Aunt Alice's bedroom. At daybreak, he was gone.

George's sorrow at watching Khalifa, Salah and the little donkey disappear out of sight didn't last for too long. There were distractions aplenty: getting reacquainted with riding Zeydoun, adjusting to his lengthening stride now that he was on flat open ground, keeping a look-out for Merlin who was bound to turn up sooner or later, and establishing a rapport with Adel, who was walking along in front, his goats grazing on the clumps of herbs as they went. Zeydoun and Lashkar kept lowering their long necks to get their fill of the readily available vegetation, which they had been deprived of in the mountains. They were in herb heaven! During the pauses whilst the animals grazed, Adel chatted to the children. George loved these interludes. She was bowled over by the shepherd boy's graceful beauty – none of the guys she knew back home were as good-looking as this one.

Fred teased his sister, making her blush. What a give-away he thought to himself! The day passed by peacefully. To please his English guests, Adel made a wild rabbit stew for their supper. To entertain them after they had eaten, he played his home-made flute, which George nick-named the magic flute, the ethereal tunes floating from this simple metal pipe causing her to drift off into a dream world of her very own...

George did not have to persuade Fred that it was time for bed – he flopped into his sleeping bag without demur, and she followed suit. Tonight, and indeed every night until they reached Sabria, they would be sleeping out in the open.

The next morning, they awoke to an overcast sky. Sitting round the campfire, munching bread dipped in olive oil, Fred was fascinated by what looked like a vast cloud of sand on the horizon. 'That could be a sandstorm coming our way,' announced Adel, who never missed a trick. He rounded up his goats, and asked Fred to keep an eye on them whilst he went off for the camels. There was a sense of urgency. George and Fred packed up their belongings ready to load onto Zeydoun and Lashkar, who were now kneeling in front of them.

Adel was impressed at how quickly George and Fred had mastered the loading and unloading routines. They had got it down to a fine art, and when he told them they were turning into real Bedouin, they felt they had well and truly earned their colours.

By 11 o'clock, the wind had whipped up into a frenzy. Sand swirled in every direction. Adel marched on resolutely, head bowed, his chech tied in such a way that only his eyes were visible. He needed to do the same for George and Fred. He couched the camels for a brief pause to count his goats and to rearrange the children's headgear. 'Thank you, Adel,' murmured George, her words fading in the roaring gale. Coherent speech was impossible. Adel checked that Lashkar was securely tied to Zeydoun. He wanted to keep going for at least another hour, by which time they should have made it across the plains to a place he knew within sight of the Sahara, where the grazing was good.

The camel train came to a standstill in front of a clump of sturdy bushes. Adel made haste. He knew that sooner rather than later visibility would be non-existent. He hobbled Zeydoun and Lashkar's front legs so that they could not wander too far away and was pleased that there was plenty for them and the goats to eat. The next thing was to set about constructing a makeshift shelter for the children and himself. He slung blankets over the bushes, knotting the corners to the bending branches which in turn, using lengths of cord, he tied to the saddle bags and jerry cans lined up in front of their temporary home. The children crawled inside, making themselves as comfortable as they could propped up against the camel saddles. Adel joined them, passing round a packet of biscuits and a mug of goat's milk. Meagre rations gratefully received, followed by a fitful siesta.

But Adel did not sleep. The sandstorm was gathering momentum. He pulled the children's sleeping bags out of the saddle bags, plus some sheep skins. There was nothing for it, but to hunker down here until the morning. He had already taken the precaution of bringing the camels closer into camp, tethering them to the bushes opposite – Zeydoun and Lashar were pale and ghostly, covered from head to toe in transient greyish-yellow mantles of sand. George and Fred peeked outside, their eyes stinging. The camels were not the only ones covered in this grainy substance.

'Fred – listen! Can you hear what I can?' Fred concentrated hard – hearing was every bit as tricky as seeing under these eerie conditions. 'Can't hear a thing, only the wind' he replied. George grabbed his arm. 'There it is again!' This time, they both heard it, a muffled squawking sound. Could it be? Was it? YES, it was! It was Merlin! The children hugged each other. And before they could say abracadabra, the bedraggled macaw had crash landed in front of them, exhausted, shivering with cold, his normally glorious blue plumage matted and muddied.

'Oh, you poor, poor bird,' cried George. 'What on earth has happened?' With some difficulty, Merlin cleared his throat. 'It is not so much about what has happened, as about what is going to happen,' he croaked. 'What do you mean by that?' piped up Fred.

'Mokhtar and Ihmed are on the warpath.'

— Chapter 27 —

İnto
the Night

Ihmed and Mokhtar were at each other's throats. They hadn't reckoned on being imprisoned in a sandstorm, and to make matters doubly hopeless, the motorbike had got a puncture.

'Why, oh why did I ever agree to take you on this wild camel chase?' remonstrated Ihmed, livid at the damage done to his bike.

'To make up for your lackadaisical police force in Djerba, who do little else but sit around on their backsides,' yelled Mokhtar. 'They're every bit as useless as this machine of yours.'

'How dare you!' screamed Ihmed. 'At least a puncture is repairable, unlike your appalling manners. Why don't you try to show some gratitude instead of hurling abuse at me.'

Their furious exchanges had been overheard by none other than Merlin, who was resting nearby in a broom bush, trying in vain to blink the sand out of his eyes. His normally sharp vision was painfully impaired. But he took comfort from his inbuilt radar system which never failed him. He simply had to follow his beak to where it took him.

George and Fred revived Merlin with a feed of dried bread and a drink of water. They hung onto every word of his report, concentrating as never before. Adel was intrigued – ignorance was bliss, but not for very much longer...

Adel listened carefully to George's French translation of the macaw's tale. He chewed on a twig and his thoughts simultaneously.

The children felt snug in their ramshackle abode, and George was especially happy that Adel was sharing it with them. So it came as a shock and something of a disappointment when he announced that after a supper of dates and milk, they were to pack, help him dismantle the camp, and ride into the night.

'But why?' asked a startled Fred. 'Can't we wait until the morning when it will be light?' George was glad that it was her brother, not her, asking these questions.

'To shake these men off, we have to get deep into the desert. Crossing what is left of the plains under the cover of darkness, whilst the wind is still blowing, plays right into our hands. We travel unseen, and the wind will blow sand over our tracks.'

'Cool,' said Fred. 'And we'll take Merlin with us – he can come with me on Lashkar.'

'George, you can do me a favour by keeping count of the goats as we go along,' added Adel. 'You'll find it much easier to see in the dark than you think.'

'Counting isn't my greatest strength, Adel, but I'll do my very best.' George was chuffed. She had just been elevated to assistant goatherd. She had never felt happier.

Supper over, it was all hands on deck. *La petite maison*, as Adel called it, collapsed in concertina-like fashion. Saddle bags were packed, camels loaded. The children wrapped up us warmly as they were able to in the few clothes they had got, and Adel tied their scarves. With a sharp knife, he cut out armholes in two of the sheepskins, turning them into instantly wearable gilets for George and Fred.

A twinge of sadness crept over George as she went to join Zeydoun. She picked up a stone from the ground. She wanted to take with her a memento from this place, which had blessed her with more than just shelter...

It was bound to be hard going, simply because they had to keep going. 'George, my legs are really hurting,' moaned Fred. 'They've been dangling for hours on end – this is the longest we've ever ridden without a break, and camel saddles don't have stirrups!'

'You're telling me, Fred! Wouldn't stirrups be a luxury! I'm in agony too. I tell you what, I'm going to ask Adel if we can walk some of the way. The ground is reasonably flat here, so I'm sure we can keep up okay, and what's more, we can go behind a bush for a pee.'

'That sounds good to me, George – I don't think I could go on much longer without giving my legs a stretch, and I've got a sore bum too.'

George spoke with Adel, who agreed to her request, provided she and Fred understood the deadline he had set himself: The Desert at Dawn, whether on foot or astride camels. Stamina was the order of the starless night.

— Chapter 28 —

The Dunes
and Douz

A pale pink sky heralded the new day. George and Fred's exhaustion turned to exhilaration – they had made it! Zeydoun and Lashkar were bouncing with glee – their nostrils filled with the sweet scent of the Sahara. Time for a well-earned rest. Adel commanded the camels to kneel, and helped the children dismount, which they did with some difficulty.

'Phew, George. I'm so stiff, and cold too.' 'Me too, Fred, but we must give Adel a hand – he wants to light a fire for us. I'm going to tell him that we'll gather the wood. He works so hard, and this is the sort of job we can easily do for him.'

The children proudly presented their trailing bundles of kindling wood to Adel. Blazing fires were lit, bread was baked, hands were warmed, mint tea was brewed. The sun rose slowly over the horizon, turning the sky pale gold. The vast sand sea was revealed in all its daunting glory.

'Goodness, George, those dunes look as though they go on forever.' 'Fear not Fred, I'm sure our ships of the desert are used to them, and with Adel at the helm, I bet it won't be that much longer before we're in Sabria. Which reminds me. I have to write a note for Merlin to take to Great Aunt Alice.'

Mokhtar and Ihmed were not as well organised as Adel and his party. They had little understanding of the rugged countryside, let alone this sandstorm which had completely flummoxed them. They had propped the motorbike up against a clump of bushes and crawled into the cramped space beneath bike and branches, where they spent an uncomfortable night.

Daylight had never been so welcome. For once, the two men forgot their differences. The puncture was irreparable. Agreed! The track ahead was unknown to them, and in any case would be obliterated by yet more sand the closer they got to the desert. Agreed! They would return to the road and the comfort of a tarmacked surface. Agreed! Taking it in turns to push the wounded bike towards the highway, they hit upon a plan – to flag down the first pickup truck that came along going in the direction of Douz. They would make this town their headquarters, buy a new tyre for the bike, and get the local police on side, whose knowledge of the locality would be invaluable.

Great Aunt Alice sat on the doorstep of Belgacem's house, enjoying an almond croissant and her morning fix of black coffee. It had been a rough old night. Douz had not escaped the storm, but now the sun shone from an azure sky. Great Aunt Alice closed her eyes, basking in the warmth. When she opened them a minute or two later, she found to her delight that she had a guest for breakfast – Merlin!

'How are you, my dear macaw, I am so pleased to see you – let me tempt you to some croissant crumbs, you must be ravenous, and dying to wash all that sand from your feathers. There's a fountain in the centre of the courtyard, which doubles as a bird bath.'

'Just what the doctor ordered, Madame Alice,' squawked Merlin repeating a phrase he often heard her use. 'But first things first – here's a note from Georgina.' His ability to pick up languages was improving by the day – soon he would be known as the multi-lingual macaw!

Feeling pleased with himself, he puffed up his feathers and released the crumpled piece of paper from his claw onto Great Aunt Alice's breakfast tray. She read, while he bathed.

'Dear Great Aunt Alice, I do hope you are well. Me, Fred and Merlin rode through the tempestuous night without a wink of sleep. We even walked some of the way. Adel is an amazing guide and gets on very well with Zeydoun and Lashkar. I've been helping him to keep a count of his goats, we call them the walking larders, as their milk keeps us alive. As I write this note, we are watching the sun rise over the Sahara – it's awesome. Soon we'll be off again. Adel says Sabria is about two days away from here.'

Great Aunt Alice poured herself another cup of coffee. She feared the children were getting a little carried away. She loved their gung-ho attitude, but this did not hide the fact that they were moving targets, with 'WANTED' over their heads. But as the rest of George's note revealed, this had not slipped her mind:

'Merlin is a wizard. He gave us the tip-off that Ihmed and Mokhtar were after us on their motorbike, so we had no time to lose, despite the sandstorm stopping them in their tracks. Adel is not one for letting the grass grow under his feet. We're so lucky to have him, and now he's going to lead us up and over the sand dunes to our destination! That's all our news for now. Lots of love, George and Fred xxxx.

PS Merlin told us you had the smoothest of drives to Douz with Belgacem, so glad, but give us camels any day, they're much more fun than trucks!'

Hmmm… mused Great Aunt Alice – that great niece of mine is a chip off the old block. Great Aunt Alice was not referring to Georgina's mother, but to herself…

Her thoughts were pleasantly interrupted. 'Good morning, Madame Alice, how are you on this beautiful day?' Belgacem had walked over from his corner shop to join his friend. It pleased him to see her so at ease in his home.

'Couldn't be better, thank you so much. Merlin has just flown in with the latest bulletin from Georgina – she and Fred seem to be having a whale of time. I just hope nothing awful happens to dampen their spirits. Ihmed and Mokhtar are hot on their trail, but the combination of a sandstorm and a puncture put paid to their cross-country pursuit.'

'That doesn't mean they are going to give up, Madame Alice. If I were in their shoes, I would hitch a lift to Douz, and hire a quad bike. Those machines make mincemeat of the desert terrain.'

George and Fred were oblivious to what might or might not be going on in Douz. George worked out a form of head gear to protect them from the searing sun. Instead of just the cotton scarf, she put on her brimmed sun hat first, and draped the scarf over and around that, tying it at the back of her neck. She did the same for her brother.

The first ride of the day was a short one to the well. George asked Adel if she and Fred could get off and wash their hands and faces in the trough. 'Yes, but camels and goats to have their drink first, please.' 'Of course,' stammered George, blushing, worried that she might have said the wrong thing.

The caravan wended its way across the rippling sands. As instructed by Adel, the children held on tightly to their saddles. But nothing could have prepared George and Fred for the stark reality of the desert. It wasn't something out of Disneyland. It was the real deal. All this space, all this sky, all this sand, and the relentless heat… They felt they were treading the surface of an alien planet, two tiny specks in a vast universe, with only the sun and the moon to remind them they were still on planet earth.

The gently sloping dunes gradually gave way to scarily steep ones. 'Don't know about you, George, but every time Lashkar struggles to reach the top of one of these, I think I'm going to slide off backwards over his tail. I have to cling on for dear life, and my arms are getting pulled out of their sockets.'

'It's the opposite for me Fred. It's clambering down the other side that gives me the heebie-jeebies. Zeydoun is so tall, and when he begins his steep descent, he lowers his head and neck almost to the ground, so that all I can see in front of me is sand. I have visions of being catapulted head-first over his shoulders, or even worse, of him falling over sideways and crushing me under his massive weight.'

Adel marched on, his bare feet sinking into the burning grains with each step, yet all the while looking back over his shoulder, making sure that George and Fred were okay.

'Please don't be afraid, George,' whispered Zeydoun in his best Noah accent. 'Lashkar and I know exactly where to place our padded feet, we've been doing it for years, ever since we were born, so don't lose faith in us, we won't let you down'. Zeydoun's comforting words, together with the concentration etched across Adel's handsome face, was all the reassurance George needed.

'We have to trust our dromedaries,' chirped Fred, 'and besides, surfing sand waves aboard their strong backs is real cool.'

'Not sure that I agree with the word cool, Fred. I'm boiling, and even the camels are sweating.'

Fred, ever protective of his sister, looked at his Swatch watch. 'It's nearly noon, George, and I read in a book somewhere that the Bedouin rest during the heat of the day.'

'I hope you're right Fred, I'm beginning to feel a bit faint.'

Adel picked up the vibes. 'In fifteen minutes' time,' he announced, 'we will be stopping at a place where the dromedaries and the goats can eat sabat.'

'What is sabat?' enquired Fred. 'Their most favourite kind of desert grass,' replied Adel. 'While the animals enjoy a lengthy lunch, we will enjoy a lengthy rest until 5 o'clock. Fred, can I rely on you to help me set up our afternoon camp?' 'You sure can' said Fred, feeling very grown up.

A leisurely afternoon spent in improvised shade, followed by an uneventful evening ride on level ground, was almost too good to be true. The sky was a magnificent melange of gold, red, and violet, changing colour by the second as the huge orange sun finally slid out of sight.

— Chapter 29 —

SOS

It was dusk when they got off their camels. George volunteered to gather wood for the fire, setting off on her own, leaving Adel and Fred to tend to the animals. A waxing moon hung suspended in the sky. She was overwhelmed by the silence of the star-studded night – no wind, no rain, not a sound to be heard. 'All is calm, all is bright,' she sang to herself, remembering the words from the Christmas carol… 'Sleep in heavenly peace, sleep in heavenly peace,' she went on.

George's head torch was a godsend, shedding light on her findings, and freeing up her hands to collect the largest armful of kindling she was capable of. She wanted to impress Adel. Pleased with her efforts, she headed back to base, and would have kept going but for a pile of brittle twigs that caught her eye. 'Might as well add these to my bundle,' she thought, as she stooped to pick them up.

A piercing scream filled the air, followed by cries for help. It was George, in some sort of trouble. Adel was gone in a trice, while poor old Fred froze, paralysed with fear.

Adel found her lying on the ground, writhing in pain. He knelt down beside her. 'I'm here, George, it's me, Adel. Please try and tell me what has happened.' But she couldn't. Her face, mouth and throat had gone numb.

A tell-tale heap of twigs gave Adel the clue he was searching for. His reaction was instantaneous. He carefully lifted the twigs with his stick, to reveal a nest of young scorpions. George had been stung. Within seconds, he had stamped them to death with the sole of his sandal.

Fred was sobbing. Zeydoun and Lashkar hobbled over to comfort him. Lashkar was the first to speak 'Look Fred – over there – can you see a torch flashing on and off?'

'Yes, I can,' said Fred, wiping the tears from his eyes. 'That's an SOS signal, something terrible must have happened!'

'Don't panic Fred, just do what I tell you,' said Zeydoun. 'Unhobble our front legs and loop the cords around our necks. These will act as neck straps to hang on to when riding bare back, which is what I am asking you to do on Lashkar.'

Fred did as he was told, and once aboard Lashkar, he flashed a response to the SOS with his own head torch, signalling that help was on its way.

There was nothing Adel could do to ease George's pain which had spread all over her body. He was desperate to get her back to camp, where he could at least make her warm and comfortable. Right now, it was a question of wait and pray.

He did not have to wait long. His prayers to Allah the Almighty were answered in the form of two shadowy shapes looming out of the darkness. Zeydoun and Lashkar had come to the rescue, carrying George's brother with them.

'Thanks Be To Allah,' murmured Adel as he watched the camels kneel, Fred clinging like a limpet to Lashkar's neck.

Fred flopped to the ground, shaking uncontrollably. Adel put his arm around him. 'So it was you Fred who saw my SOS and signalled back.' 'Yes,' sobbed Fred. 'But please, please tell me George is alright. I want to talk to her.'

'George is very poorly, Fred. She's been stung by a scorpion.'

'Does that mean she'll die?' blurted Fred. 'Scorpions can kill you, can't they? Promise me she'll be okay. Life without George wouldn't be worth living.'

'Shoosh, Fred, keep your voice down. George mustn't hear you talking like that. She is not going to die, Inshallah, but we have to get a move on. She's shivering with fear and cold. You are to ride Zeydoun back to camp. I've loaded George's bundle of wood onto him, and I will take George with me, on Lashkar.'

Adel lifted a petrified Fred onto Zeydoun – he had never ridden such a huge camel and didn't want to make a fool of himself. 'Don't be scared, Fred,' whispered Zeydoun. 'I will look after you, and Lashkar will take good care of George and Adel – look – they're on his back already.'

The camels were on autopilot, retracing their tracks. Allah's blessings were infinite that night. A lone camel herder awaited their return. 'Salam Alaikum, Adel!' It was Saleem, Adel's uncle! 'Alaikum-Salaam, Saleem, Alaikum-Salaam!'

Saleem took over, leaving Adel to nurse George. A sensitive soul, and a natural with children (he had five of his own) he could see that traumatised Fred needed every bit as much attention as his sister, albeit in a different form. 'Hello Fred, I'm Adel's uncle. There is much work to be done tonight. Can you give me a hand, please?' Saleem's smiling face and twinkling eyes cheered Fred up no end. 'I'd love to,' he smiled back.

— Chapter 30 —

Market
Day

Market day in Douz was a 21st century social gathering, or a scene straight out of the Old Testament. It was a mix of both. A perspiring Belgacem ushered a respectfully be-scarved Great Aunt Alice through the throng of farmers, camel herders, shepherds, horsemen, mule and donkey drivers, all seeking the best prices they could get for their livestock, produce and wares. A milling crowd of men and women, dressed in traditional flowing Bedouin robes, jostled under the shade of the palm trees, exchanging gossip and dinars at the top of their voices. She couldn't quite put her finger on it, but for some reason or other, Great Aunt Alice began to feel apprehensive.

Ihmed and Mokhtar emerged showered and well fed from their overnight lodgings, Ihmed in police uniform. Everything so far had gone to plan. A truck driver had given them a lift to Douz the day before, dropping them off at a grimy garage specialising in motorbike tyres; the mechanic there had recommended a small hotel in Avenue Mars, owned by a friend of his called Jamal, who obligingly gave Ihmed a map of Douz on which the police station was clearly marked. The two men found their way to the whitewashed building. The red Tunisian national flag, sporting a star and crescent, fluttered above the entrance. Ihmed was warmly welcomed by the officer on duty who handed him a cigarette. 'Thank you, but I don't smoke,' said Ihmed, trying not to sound ungrateful. 'But my colleague does.' Mokhtar did not hesitate. Half an hour and several cigarettes later, Mokhtar's tale of woe drew to an inconclusive end.

'Ihmed, you are in luck,' announced the police officer, stifling a yawn. 'The timing for you and your friend couldn't be better. Today is market day. Keep your eyes and ears open. My duty is to issue formal notice of this theft to every police station within the Kebili region, stating the alleged culprits are two children, a girl and a boy. Your duty is to report back to me with any relevant information which enables us to take the matter further.' Ihmed and Mokhtar thanked the officer for his assistance, and, pleased with their morning's work, took themselves off to a noisy corner street café where they feasted on skewered camel meat kebabs. 'Even if I never find my own camels, I'm at least going to enjoy eating these ones,' quipped Mokhtar, laughing at his own joke.

Great Aunt Alice had never been one for livestock markets. In England they were bad enough, but over here they were far worse. It distressed her to see bewildered animals being manhandled into pens, where they stood helplessly awaiting their fate in the heat. Up until this moment, she had been mesmerized by the sheer vibrancy of the colourful stalls selling spices, vegetables, fruits, and fabrics, but they had given way to bleak cages crammed with panting chickens and forlorn lop-eared rabbits. Great Aunt Alice decided there and then to buy six chickens and two rabbits as pets for Belgacem's household. The vendor bundled them into cardboard boxes tied with string, and handed them to his glamorous client, pleased with his first sale of the day.

'Let me help you, Madame Alice,' offered Belgacem, taking the boxes from her. 'You make me and my children very happy.' 'And these poor creatures too, I hope!' smiled Great Aunt Alice.

It was on their walk back to Belgacem's pickup truck that they passed the section of the market that Great Aunt Alice had taken such a dislike to. Here men shouted, spat and brandished sticks, hitting their wretched animals when they had nothing better to do. It was the lowly donkeys and mules who bore the brunt of the blows. The camels fared better, as did the majority of the horses – they were the revered beasts of burden, mostly belonging to kind, caring owners who had never wanted to sell their treasured animals in the first place.

Mokhtar and Ihmed must have missed Great Aunt Alice by a matter of moments, arriving at the pens just after she had left. Mokhtar sat down on an up-turned crate and lit another cigarette. Somebody tapped him on the shoulder. 'Come to buy more camels, have you? Must be more tourists in Djerba than we've got in Douz.' Mokhtar was flabbergasted. Standing in front of him was the very same dealer who had sold him Zeydoun and Lashkar.

Mokhtar jumped to his feet, his voice cracking with emotion. 'The answer to your first question is a NO, but to your second one, a YES.' 'So what brings you down here?' ventured the dealer. 'Those were two fine camels I sold you – nothing wrong I hope?'

'Only that they've been stolen by children. I've been made to look a complete fool.' He paused to take a deep breath. 'Care for a cigarette?' The puzzled dealer accepted. He couldn't believe what he was hearing. 'Well at least you've got the police onto it,' he remarked.

'Yes, that's me, Ihmed, a friend of Mokhtar's, now acting in my official capacity as well, that is until the mystery of the missing camels has been solved. Did I overhear you saying that it was you who originally sold them to Mokhtar?'

'Yes,' replied the dealer. Ihmed turned to Mokhtar, grinning from ear to ear 'We've struck gold, my friend. This good man should be able to tell us exactly where Zeydoun and Lashkar came from.

Once we know that, we can put a plan into action'. 'Of course, I can tell you,' the dealer butted in. 'They came from Sabria, a small oasis just twenty miles away.'

Merlin was too wise to allow market day to pass him by. All morning he had been stalking Ihmed and Mokhtar. His perseverance was rewarded. Concealed in a leafy pomegranate bush, he listened in to their conversation with the dealer. There was no time to lose. He must get word to Great Aunt Alice post-haste before winging his way back to the desert.

— Chapter 31 —

The
Camera

'Adel, I need to go to the loo again, please. Can you come with me, just like you did during the night? I'm still too frightened to go behind a bush all by myself in case there are more scorpions.' Adel had kept vigil over his fragile friend throughout the long hours of darkness, never leaving her side.

He held her hand in his. 'Don't be afraid George. I'm here for you, always.' The first streaks of dawn were breaking across the horizon. Adel escorted George to a broom bush, and having cast his eye over the surrounding ground, discreetly turned the other way.

Fred woke up with a start. Where was George? Where was Adel? What has happened?

'Morning Fred!' beamed Saleem. 'No need to panic. George has recovered, all is well. She's just gone on a little walk with Adel to stretch her legs. Come and warm your hands by the fire. Breakfast is ready, and so are the camels. You are going to make an extra early start today, as Adel is aiming to reach Sabria by nightfall.' 'Gosh,' said Fred. 'Will George be up to it?' 'Why don't you ask her yourself, Fred, she's standing right behind you.'

138

And so she was! Brother and sister fell into each other's arms. 'Are you really okay, George? Am I happy to see you on your feet again!' exclaimed Fred, giving his sister a big hug.

'Apart from the sore place on my hand where the venomous scorpion stung me,' explained George, pointing to the wound, 'I'm feeling pretty good, thanks to Adel's expertise – he makes a terrific nurse! He tore off a length of cloth from his chech, soaked it in cold water, and supplied me with endless cold packs throughout the night to soothe the sting. At first, I thought he was going to make a tourniquet, but no, he told me those can do more harm than good.'

Saleem brewed camomile tea for the children and produced honey for them to enjoy with their bread. 'Wow, what a treat, Saleem,' said Fred. 'Yes,' seconded George. 'Thank you, dear Saleem, we've got a big day ahead, and this scrummy breakfast will get us off to a cracking start. Thank you too for being so kind to Fred.'

The children made doubly sure they hadn't left anything behind before hitching their rucksacks to the front of their saddles. They now waited for Adel and Saleem, who had gone off to gather up the goats. The pitter patter of hooves announced their return.

The time had come for the children to be helped onto Zeydoun and Lashkar. They braced themselves for another goodbye – this time from Saleem. Deeply moved by their courage, he took their hands into his. 'Bon voyage, mes enfants, may Allah be with you.'

'I can't bear these partings,' said George. 'They get harder and harder'. 'I feel exactly the same, if that makes it any better,' consoled Fred. For Adel though, the formal hellos and goodbyes were part of the Bedouin tradition. He kissed his uncle on both cheeks, did a quick head count of the goats, looped the rope attached to Zeydoun's nostril around his wrist, and was off.

In spite of a sleepless night, Adel was clearheaded. He planned to complete the longest leg of the journey during the earliest part of the day. Yes, there would be regular pauses, but no lolling about at midday, however hot the sun. The camel train had to keep on the move, especially as it was quite possible that George could suffer a delayed reaction to the scorpion sting, in which case she would be better off in Sabria where the Bedouin women could nurse her. The weather was on their side – a cool breeze rippled over the white sands, and a scattering of fluffy clouds kept the sun at bay. To boost the children's morale, Adel would often break into mellifluous song as he zig-zagged his way up, over, down and around the dunes. George was enchanted.

'Don't you think he's got the most beautiful voice you've ever heard, Fred?' But before Fred could answer, a squawking Merlin swooped onto Lashkar's neck. 'I am the bearer of bad tidings,' he croaked, his throat parched after flying into the wind. 'Mokhtar has met up with the dealer who sold him Zeydoun and Lashkar. He now knows where they came from!' George's dream world was shattered in a split second by the stark reality that faced them: What if Mokhtar were to reclaim his camels and take them all the way back to Djerba? After all her and Fred's efforts to liberate them?

Ihmed strutted into the police station, accompanied by Mokhtar and the dealer. Statements were made to the officer on duty, who took down notes as he listened. Eventually it was his turn to speak.

'My advice would be for you and Mokhtar to stay in the ancient fort on the outskirts of Sabria, which is run as a hotel. Make this your headquarters, and bide your time. My next piece of advice is to hire a quad bike – the garage opposite has just invested in some brand-new ones. They are the best vehicles for the Sahara and will take you anywhere. They are very popular with the tourists.'

Meanwhile, on the other side of town, Great Aunt Alice and Belgacem sat in silence, Belgacem with his head in his hands. The lunch Aisha had prepared for them remained untouched. Great Aunt Alice was the first to speak.

'I've just remembered – Georgina's camera! Let me go and fetch it from my room.'

Great Aunt Alice rose to her feet. Getting up from the rush matted floor was not the easiest of tasks, but one she handled with the utmost elegance. Within minutes, she was back again.

'Here, let me show you'. Belgacem was shocked at what the camera revealed. One after the other, tragic photographs slid across the screen. He was ashamed. How could anyone treat camels like this? What would Madame Alice think of the Tunisian people? But Great Aunt Alice had already thought.

'Belgacem, please take me to the nearest shop that specialises in photography. I want to get these photos developed into the largest colour prints they can manage – preferably poster size.' A fountain of all knowledge, he knew of just the place. Great Aunt Alice left the camera in the capable hands of the shopkeeper who happened to be a friend of Belgacem's. 'He will do a good job for you, Madame Alice. He says we are to come back in two hours by which time your prints and camera will be ready for collection.' Great Aunt Alice paid the shopkeeper there and then. She never ventured anywhere without a wodge of notes about her person.

'Let us go back to the house Madame Alice and enjoy our couscous – we can eat at leisure while we wait for the photographs, and between us decide what we do next. I already have something in mind.' Great Aunt Alice's appetite returned. She had every faith in the wily Belgacem, and a useful trick up her own sleeve.

Chapter 32

Matoumatheni

B elgacem bundled blankets into the pickup, while Great Aunt Alice packed a few things into her straw basket – a minimalist amount of toiletries, a change of underwear, and a warm sweater.

'After we've collected your camera and photographs, we'll fill the pickup with petrol, and drive to Matoumatheni,' announced Belgacem. 'You are about to experience your first night in the Tunisian Sahara, Madame Alice.'

Great Aunt Alice was thrilled. Some years ago, she had travelled across the Malian Sahara under the care and protection of the Touareg, and here she was in Tunisia, embarking on another desert adventure, this time with the nomadic Bedouin. It is this tribe's springtime tradition to leave their settled villages for several weeks, taking their livestock with them to graze on the tender young shoots of herbs, shrubs, and grass.

'Madame Alice, Matoumatheni is a wondrous place on high ground overlooking Sabria. You will meet many Bedouin families enjoying the freedom of nomadic life, swapping their brick houses for tents woven from sheep, camel and goat hair. We will join my brother-in-law Waheed and his family. They bring their chickens with them, so you can be sure of a fresh egg for your breakfast.'

'Sounds delightful, my dear Belgacem, but where do George and Fred fit into this idyllic scenario?'

'Trust me, Madame Alice, I know what I am doing. We will be inconspicuous, part of the convivial gathering, and, dressed respectfully as you always are, you will be treated as one of us, not as a tourist. Besides, you are my guest. From the safety of the encampment with its panoramic view, we can watch the comings and goings all around us, which means, Inshallah, we should be able to see Zeydoun and Lashkar's homecoming, and most importantly, keep a sharp lookout for Mokhtar and Ihmed. It will be my decision when to lie low, and when to make a move. Timing is of the essence.'

The two-seater quad bike hurtled towards Sabria, Ihmed at the wheel, until suddenly the men found themselves vaulting into the air. They had hit the first of the great bumps in the road designed to slow traffic down – ironically, these bumps are known as sleeping policemen.

'Steady on,' shouted Mokhtar as they lurched back into their seats. The village of Zaafrane was fast approaching, and the sleeping policemen intervened again. But Ihmed was like a child with a new toy. Nothing was going to stop him.

'Look out,' yelled Mokhtar as a black cat darted into the middle of the street. But Ihmed kept going, running over the helpless feline without giving it a second thought. 'You fool,' screamed Mokhtar, 'that wasn't very clever. Black cats bring good luck. Killing one will bring us bad luck.'

'You might be superstitious Mokhtar, but I'm not, never have been. At least I've done the mouse population a good turn – one less predator for them to worry about. Look on the bright side my friend, we'll soon be in Sabria – I'll buy you a beer when we get to Le Fort Hotel – if they've got any.'

Merlin ruffled his glossy blue feathers. Perched on Lashkar's curved neck, he was getting ready to courier George's latest message to Great Aunt Alice before it got dark. During the day's ride, he had made a couple of reconnaissance flights. He was so grateful that Lashkar provided the perfect landing pad each time he got back – not so much a ship of the desert as an aircraft carrier.

Tonight's flight was a short one. Great Aunt Alice and Belgacem were nearby. Merlin collected George's missive which she had scribbled in a fever of excitement:

'Dear Great Aunt Alice

We're almost there! We'll be spending the night in Sabria! We can just make out the silhouetted date palms in the oasis, but it's getting dark very quickly. The camels are bouncing with happiness, and so are we! Can you please get to the village as early as you can tomorrow? Do hope you're not too cross with us. Sorry if you've been worried, but it has been so worth it, I promise. You'll see for yourself tomorrow. Please say hi to Belgacem.

Hugs and kisses, George and Fred xxxx'

Merlin landed on the bamboo fence surrounding Waheed's tent. He dropped George's note into his mistress's lap. 'How good to see you Merlin. Can you please wait while I read what my Great Niece has to say, so that I can write a reply for you to take straight back to her?'

'My Darlings

How lovely to hear from you. Belgacem and I will be with you first thing in the morning. We are well prepared. We need to be – I have to warn you that Mokhtar and Ihmed have beaten you to it. We hear they are already in the village, staying at Le Fort Hotel.

Fondest love, your Great Aunt Alice'

Under the silvery light of the waxing moon, Merlin flew to Sabria, holding Great Aunt Alice's note in his beak.

— Chapter 33 —

The Day
of Reckoning

'Good morning, Madame Alice, your chariot awaits.' Great Aunt Alice rose to her feet, fully clothed. It was the Bedouin custom to go to bed in whatever one had worn during the day. Careful not to disturb Waheed's slumbering family in their communal tent, Belgacem and Great Aunt Alice stepped carefully over the sleeping bodies and out into the chilly morning air to make their acquaintance with the chocolate brown donkey standing patiently between the shafts, his head bowed. 'We will not attract any local attention arriving in Waheed's donkey-drawn chariot – the comings and goings from Sabria at this time of year are all part of springtime's rich tapestry.'

Adel and his party had spent the night concealed amongst row upon row of palm trees in the oasis. The morning could not come soon enough for both children and camels. Clearly sleep was impossible. Zeydoun and Lashkar were barely able to contain their excitement, but poor old George and Fred were feeling jangled after reading Great Aunt Alice's latest note. They snuggled up to the resting camels for warmth and comfort. Setting up camp was not an option tonight. Adel kept watch over his goats, his bernous wrapped tightly around him.

His long eyelashes glistening with tears of relief, it was Zeydoun who thought to fill these moonlit hours with some story telling: 'Tomorrow you will see my village in daylight,' he proudly declared to George and Fred in his deep velvety voice, his tummy all the while making rumbling noises. 'Let me tell you what to expect – a lively mixture of people and animals – women going about their daily chores, children playing, men on their way to pray at the mosque, men drinking tea outside the cafés, sheep, goats, donkeys, mules, horses, and camels, penned or tethered.'

'Are there any shops?' asked George. 'And what about pavements?' interrupted Fred. 'Shops, yes,' replied Zeydoun, 'selling basic provisions. Pavements, no. Just a maze of sandy streets and alleyways running between one storied red brick houses, most with flat roofs and shuttered windows. Some of the dwellings have running water now.'

'Goodness,' said George, 'and what about loos?' She hadn't seen one of these for days! 'You'll be pleased to hear that Khairi's house has one, and a shower too,' comforted Zeydoun. 'What luxury' cooed George at the thought of warm water. Zeydoun continued: 'When the village awakes, Lashkar and I will lead you to his house. You, Fred, Adel and the goats are to follow us. We mustn't forget Merlin – we could so easily lose him amongst all these trees and crops – lucky his feathers are blue and gold, and not the same bright green as the lucerne growing underfoot.' 'Indeed,' squawked Merlin, who had no intention of getting left behind.

Mokhtar had never been one for early mornings, not even in a crisis. To his delight, Le Fort Hotel housed crates of beer in a cave behind the bar. Temptation had got the better of him, and surprisingly, Ihmed too. Both men had snored the night away in a drunken stupor, losing valuable time, unlike the other characters in our story, all of whom were well ahead of the game.

Not so Khairi and his family, who had no idea of what had been going on these past few days. But an unexpected knock on their front door was about to change everything. What Khairi saw next shook him to the core. Kneeling in homage to their beloved former master were Zeydoun and Lashkar – there was no mistaking them, in spite of their rather peculiar colours. And who were these children? Adel stepped forward, but Khairi cut the formal greetings short.

'What in Allah's name is going on? I exchanged these camels for money – I had to – and yet here they are back again. I can't afford to buy them back, and now I stand to be accused of stealing them.'

Khairi's little boy, Neo, came running out of the house and patted the camels on their soft noses. He had missed them so much! 'Papa, Mama, my furry friends have come home!' George and Fred looked on in bewilderment whilst Adel did his best to put over their epic tale to Khairi in Arabic. It had never entered their heads that they could have landed the dromedaries' original owner into a massive amount of trouble. All they longed for was a happy ending for everyone.

Meanwhile, Belgacem tapped the little donkey gently on its neck. Ears pricked, away it went at a steady trot along the desert track leading to Sabria. Great Aunt Alice's boiled egg would have to wait until their return to Matoumatheni – if all went well, the children would be joining them for a celebratory breakfast.

They passed Le Fort Hotel on the outskirts of Sabria and pulled up at the village well to fill the empty plastic containers with fresh water for Waheed. Great Aunt Alice did not feel at her best sitting on the flat-bottomed chariot with her legs dangling over the side. But any thoughts of how she looked soon evaporated in the deafening roar of an engine, causing the little donkey to veer sideways. A quad bike sped past, creating a mini sandstorm in its wake. With some difficulty, Great Aunt Alice managed to keep her balance. Belgacem, already on the ground, steadied the little donkey. 'Madame Alice, we do not make a move until the dust has settled. For sure, the riders on that bike are Ihmed and Mokhtar.'

The bike was forced to slow down as it approached the far end of the sandy street. Children had gathered to play, and women were getting their horses and carts harnessed in readiness for a morning's work scything lucerne in the oasis. But they were distracted by what they saw outside Khairi's house: Two kneeling camels, two children – a boy and a girl dressed in western clothes, a young Bedouin shepherd trying to prevent his herd of goats from straying, and an extraordinary-looking blue and gold feathered bird swaying to and fro on a line of washing, hung out to dry in the morning sun. An animated conversation was going on between Khairi and the shepherd boy. This unusual scene was made all the more so by the arrival of a quad bike with a uniformed police officer in the driving seat, a dishevelled passenger clinging on to him with one hand, holding a cigarette in the other.

Ihmed switched off the engine. 'Time for us to make ourselves known, my friend,' he smirked. 'We've got the culprits cornered, children, shepherd, goats, camels, parrot and all. Let's give them the fright of their lives.' A twisted smile crossed Mokhtar's face, exposing his ugly tobacco-stained teeth.

Khairi's wife Chiraz stepped out of the house, her arm around their tearful son. 'What is going on Khairi? What are Zeydoun and Lashkar doing here – and these children?'

'I'll tell you what,' butted in Ihmed as he swaggered through the curious crowd. 'These camels are the property of my friend Mokhtar, and these two children are the thieves. They are under immediate arrest, as is the shepherd. I will arrange for a truck to take the stolen dromedaries back to Djerba, dropping off the boy, girl and that ridiculous bird at the Douz police station. A tractor and trailer will bring along the shepherd and his flock to join us for the interrogation. But first I must question

Khairi to see if he played any part in this crime. If that is the case, he will bring shame upon the whole village of Sabria.'

Ihmed was so carried away by the power he and his uniform portrayed that he was unaware of two notable spectators who had joined the crowd: Belgacem and Great Aunt Alice. 'Steady on officer,' said Belgacem calmly. 'These children must be allowed their say in this matter, and Mokhtar has to formally identify his dromedaries.' Mokhtar took his time – the black camel had turned a pinkish grey, and the white one's coat was covered in terracotta blotches. 'They're mine alright. I can tell from the brand marks on their cheeks and hind quarters.'

Up until now, Great Aunt Alice hadn't spoken a word. 'Good morning, officer. May I introduce myself. I am responsible for these two children, Georgina and Freddie. I am their Great Aunt.'

'That may be, Madame, but it makes little difference to the crime they have committed,' responded Ihmed.

'I realise you are only doing your job, officer, but what I am about to show you tells another side of the story.' George and Fred looked anxiously at one another, as if to say, 'what next?' Great Aunt Alice proceeded to hand three rolled-up posters tied with red ribbon to Ihmed. 'May I ask you to please have a look at these – not a pretty sight, as I am sure you will agree.' One by one, Ihmed studied them. Although no animal lover himself, he knew only too well that dromedaries are held in high esteem by most Tunisians, who would be shocked to see these blown up photographs illustrating bleeding saddle sores, blistered mouths, sticking out ribs, and rough lack-lustre coats infested with blood sucking ticks. Their forelegs bore the marks of where the hobble ropes had been tied so tightly that the skin had been rubbed raw, almost down to the bone.

'Where did these photographs come from Madame?' Great Aunt Alice held up the children's yellow camera. 'From here,' she answered. Mokhtar looked uneasy. He had never cared about the animals' welfare, only that they were a source of income, earning him money by providing tourists with endless camel rides up and down the beach, as many as he could cram into each hour.

Belgacem broke the uncomfortable silence. 'How would Mokhtar like to see these posters slapped up in Djerba – I have found out that a well-known animal charity, dedicated to rescuing cruelly treated working animals, has recently opened an office in Tunis – it would most certainly want to get its hands on these two beasts, and to see Mokhtar severely punished for his misdoings. Yet here you are, officer, seeking to punish two children who in their innocence took it upon themselves to do what they thought was right – to liberate two desperately treated animals from their sadistic owner.' Things were not going as well for Ihmed as he had hoped. Great Aunt Alice put in a word for him.

'Officer, there is no denying that in the eyes of the law, these children have committed the crime of theft, for which they are answerable. I completely understand that it is your duty to uphold the law of the land, but might I ask you to reflect upon those photographs you have in your possession. You may keep them to show to your superiors. I have copies for my own records.'

No sooner had Great Aunt Alice spoken than a police car drew up outside Khairi's house, its wheels spinning in the sand. For one ghastly moment, she had visions of George and Fred being taken away. Two policemen jumped out and made straight for the riderless quad bike.

'Yes, this is the vehicle that did it,' shouted the senior police officer to his junior. 'Please take a photograph and make a note of any relevant details while I go and officially charge the rider with a speeding offence, and the wilful killing of my grandmother's black cat. We have a silent witness: Zaafrane's close circuit TV Camera. This incident may seem trivial, but when committed by a fellow officer, is very serious indeed.'

Ihmed was taking a closer look at the posters. 'What have you got there?' enquired the senior officer as he made himself known to Ihmed. Mokhtar cringed.

'Good news sir. I've finally caught up with the juvenile thieves who made it their business to ride two camels from Djerba to Sabria. They have the nerve to interpret their actions as a rescue operation, not a crime. These beasts happen to be the property of my friend here,' he added, pointing a finger at Mokhtar.

'Hmm,' muttered the senior officer, who had indeed read the notices offering a reward to anyone who could assist the police with their enquiries. He twirled his moustache thoughtfully. 'I did not come here expecting to find the stolen camels, though that is certainly a bonus. The purpose of my visit to Sabria is to charge you with an offence, namely speeding through a built-up area, and causing wilful damage. But perhaps most serious of all is the fact that you have brought our law-abiding profession into disrepute.' Ihmed's face fell, Mokhtar's even further.

Great Aunt Alice took Belgacem to one side. She had picked up the gist of the policeman's conversation with Ihmed but wanted to be sure of the facts. She asked her translator-in-chief for the English version. Belgacem obliged. Great Aunt Alice took in every word. Now it was his turn to listen to what Madame Alice wanted him to convey to the senior police officer on her behalf.

Great Aunt Alice was astute when it came to a deal. She was, after all, a horse dealer's daughter, and had on many an occasion watched her dear, late father shaking hands with the prospective buyer once the bartering was over, and a final figure mutually agreed. 'Belgacem, I cannot overrule Ihmed's speeding offence. But I can compensate Mokhtar for the loss of his camels, and the expenses he has notched up in his endeavours to find them, which might include Ihmed's statutory speeding fine. Can you please suggest that rather than accusing Georgina and Freddie of theft, that they should be commended for their bravery in liberating two dromedaries from a ruthlessly cruel owner. To make up for Mokhtar's loss of earnings, I am prepared to buy him a brand-new quad bike of his choice from my garage in Djerba, with which he can do as he pleases, and in addition, give him a lump sum in cash, which we will work out between us.'

Belgacem nodded and proceeded to carry out Great Aunt Alice's instructions to the letter. The senior police officer respected her proposals, even more so after he had had the chance to scrutinize the blown-up photographs. 'Mokhtar, you have nothing to lose and all to gain from this good lady's offer. My suggestion is that you take it.' He did. The deal was done.

— Chapter 34 —

The
Final Ride

Khairi, Chiraz and Neo joined Great Aunt Alice on the flat-bottomed chariot. Belgacem took up the reins, and the little donkey braced himself for the uphill trek to Matoumatheni, his load three people and several containers of water heavier than earlier. Zeydoun and Lashkar knew their way to the springtime camp, leaving Adel free to roam with his grazing goats – he would catch up with Great Aunt Alice in time for the celebratory breakfast, and had accepted her kind invitation gladly. It was the first time in days that Adel found himself alone, and he was not sure if he liked it.

George and Fred could not believe what they had achieved, and neither could Great Aunt Alice who knew only too well the reaction the children would suffer when they had to finally part with their dromedaries.

'Do you realise this is our final ride, Fred – the very last time we will be on our camels – I can't bear to think about it.' 'Neither can I,' agreed Fred, as Lashkar lowered his neck to feast on the spring grasses. The children were in no hurry to get to the encampment. They were dreading their journey's end.

'It's strange not having Adel leading the way, isn't it George?' But she didn't answer. 'Are you okay, George?'

'Not sure,' came her barely audible reply.

'Is it just the thought of saying goodbye to the camels that's making you sad, George, or is it something else?' probed Fred gently, not wanting to upset his sister further.

'It's everything Fred. I don't ever want go back to England. I'm so happy in Tunisia, and Great Aunt Alice is such a good sport. Mum and Dad aren't nearly as much fun, and then there's weeks and weeks of the summer term to get through.'

'That's life, George – just like our incredible adventure – full of ups and downs. Our parents were so clever in the first place to send us to Great Aunt Alice for our Easter holidays.'

'Yes, I suppose so, Fred, and I do love them very much, just as I love you. But I have also grown to love the mountains, the desert and all the dear people we have met along the way. If it hadn't been for them, we'd never have made it to Sabria, and then there was dear Lotfi the fisherman and his friend Sharif. Each and every one of them has risked life, limb and livelihood in helping us to return Zeydoun and Lashkar to their rightful home.'

Merlin had chosen to perch between Zeydoun's ears for the triumphant march into Matoumatheni. He had listened to George and Fred chattering away to each other with an attentive ear. Wise bird that he was, he knew that George hadn't revealed all her innermost thoughts to her brother.

Adel sat on a rock and got out his flute. His slender fingers danced as he played, but the tune came from deep within his heart. He envied the swooping swallows around him. They were clever enough to fly to England and back again once the hot African summer months had passed. Why couldn't he be like them? He was going to miss George, Fred and the camels dreadfully, George especially. What could he give her as a keepsake? A goat jumped on to the rocks beside him, a handsome chestnut one. He plucked a handful of hair from the thickest part of its long shiny coat and began plaiting it into the shape of a heart.

Great Aunt Alice knew she must have a serious talk with Khairi before they got to Waheed's tent, where there would be no privacy. She had the added advantage of having Belgacem as her interpreter. 'Khairi, I need to put your mind at rest. First and foremost, the police are satisfied that you played no part in the theft of the camels. They have accepted that these animals were liberated, not stolen, from their appalling existence by my great niece and nephew. I accept complete responsibility for George and Fred's actions, and I whole-heartedly stand by them. Last, but not least, I assure you of my on-going commitment to Zeydoun and Lashkar. I shall send you money each month for their keep and care. I have some challenging long-term plans in mind too, but more of that later.'

The joys of springtime in Matoumatheni were familiar to Zeydoun and Lashkar. 'We hope you'll love this magical place as much as we do,' enthused Lashkar to Fred. 'We never thought we'd be part of this Bedouin tradition again. But we are, all thanks to you and George, and your steadfast faith in us.' As they crested the last of the undulating white dunes, there below them lay a patchwork of broom bushes, flowering shrubs, clumps of herbs and tufts of grass. Interspersed amongst the sand and verdant vegetation were the hand-woven Bedouin tents. Plumes of smoke rose from the campfires, and women dressed in brightly coloured ankle length kaftans with headscarves to match, watched their children play in the sunshine.

'Look George, there's Great Aunt Alice – that must be Belgacem's brother-in-law's tent.' 'You're right Fred! Zeydoun, Lashkar, behold our Saviour! Only Great Aunt Alice could have made our adventure turn out alright.'

The camels padded regally towards Waheed's tent, their heads held high. Great Aunt Alice was standing at the entrance, Khairi and Chiraz at her side. Zeydoun and Lashkar knelt at their feet. Merlin flew to the ground. George and Fred dismounted for the final time, not quite knowing how to manage their emotions. George turned to look back at the dunes. Adel and his herd were wandering slowly towards her.

'Great Aunt Alice, do you mind if I walk over to meet Adel? It's not that far, and I need to stretch my legs.'

'Of course not, darling George, that's a splendid idea.'

— Chapter 35 —

The Parting
of the Ways

Skinny lizards slithered across George's path. Birdsong filled the crystal-clear morning air. Butterflies, bees and the occasional dragonfly hovered over the delicately scented flowering shrubs. The sun radiated warmth from a cloudless blue sky. It was a perfect day, with so much to celebrate. But for George and Adel, the beauty of the day only accentuated the agony of their imminent parting. Sharing the joys of spring would all too soon be a thing of the past.

Adel was counting his herd, a task he had so often delegated to George. 'Good morning, dearest goatherd. What am I going to do without you, and how am I going to keep my goats in order?'

'Like you've always done,' she replied bravely, 'though it can never be quite the same.'

George's eyes filled with tears. Adel wiped them away with the folds of his chech. When she looked up at him, she saw that his lower lip was trembling.

'It's going to be hard for us both, George. But I promise I will never forget you. Ever. To make sure of that, I bought a leather collar and copper bell from the blacksmith in Khairi's village. My prettiest goat wears it around her neck - listen!' George listened. 'Every time I hear that bell, I shall think of you, my friend. Now, shut your eyes and hold out your hand.' George did as she was told.

Into her outstretched palm, he placed the plaited heart, whispering 'Toujours dans mon coeur, dear, sweet George, toujours dans mon coeur.'

— Author's Note —

Make no mistake, Great Aunt Alice is really me, and I really do own a black camel. I keep him with my Bedouin friends in the Tunisian Sahara and have done so for the past thirteen years. We are growing old together.

My story is a fictionalised memoir, woven around fact, of an English woman's adventures with her dromedary. Everything is based on my own experiences, and the people I have met. Strangely enough, I've always been fascinated by camels and have ridden them all over the world:

Mali, Mongolia, Morocco, Kenya, Egypt, Jordan, Syria, Oman, Australia, and in India (the only time I fell off a camel).

A horse dealer's daughter, I was brought up with horses and a love of the great outdoors. These formative years undoubtedly played their part in my choice of holiday destinations throughout my secretarial career in London. To escape the restraints of an office environment (which included twelve years assisting the General Manager of The Savoy Hotel) I opted to travel in countries where I could spend twenty-four hours a day out in the open air, surrounded by animals and those that looked after them. The deserts, combined with the resilience of the camels and the local knowledge of the nomadic tribesmen, were my idea of utopia.

It was on New Year's Day 2008, that I bought my very own Algerian bred camel Zeydoun, a black stallion. Ever since that momentous day, I have ridden him across the Saharan sands three or four times a year, often taking like-minded friends and family with me, including George and Fred on two occasions. Not only have we enjoyed great fun, laughter and camaraderie, but we have also been able to bring much-needed work to the Bedouin who depend so much upon the fragile tourism industry.

To see my story in print is a dream come true, for which I have to thank my friends at The Garrick Club Piers Pottinger, Geoffrey Wansell, John Rawnsley and James Hogan. One introduction inevitably leads to another, and it was James who introduced me to George Spender and Konstantinos Vasdekis of the publisher Salamander Street. But it was serendipity that brought my illustrator, Mia Buckton, to me. We met on the No.38 bus travelling from Bloomsbury to Pimlico. You have all played a crucial part in making *Great Aunt Alice and the Black Camel* happen.

I would like to thank my many friends and fellow travellers for all their encouragement, and for taking some of the photographs in this book.

Diana Fletcher
London, February 2021

— The Author —

Diana Fletcher's working career embraced being secretary to the General Manager of the Savoy Hotel London, and secretary to one of the two named partners of the renowned public relations firm Bell Pottinger. Born in Somerset, the daughter of a farmer, she has always loved to travel, especially when working in high pressured jobs. She wanted to get as far away from the telephone as possible. Those journeys took her all over the world, and on the way Diana developed a passion for camels, a passion that saw her purchase her own black camel stallion thirteen years ago. This is her first book.

Lightning Source UK Ltd.
Milton Keynes UK
UKHW050952170921
390725UK00003B/14